ADVANCE PRAISE

LUNGS OF MY E

CW00821867

"Hauntingly beautiful. An intimate, lyrical, brave, unabashedly heartfelt account of what it feels like to be alive in the world, the pulsing, breathing, living world. In language reminiscent of Jean Giono and Gerard Manley Hopkins, Searle helps us feel (again) the immersive, porous, ecstatic character of our life in the company of other living beings. A wonderful gift."
—Douglas Christie, author of *The Blue Sapphire of the Mind: Notes for a Contemplative Ecology*

≈

"William Henry Searle guides us through six particular landscapes, richly described and wisely reflected upon. As we journey through forests, marshlands and wind-scoured mountains, we discover what modern humans are most starved for: an embodied connection with a numinous world. This lyrical and potent book deserves a permanent place in the bookshelves of anyone interested in bridging the false divide between outer and inner nature, Earth and soul."
—Mary Reynolds Thompson, Author of *Embrace Your Inner Wild: 52 Reflections for an Eco-Centric World* and *Reclaiming the Wild Soul: How Earth's Landscapes Restore Us to Wholeness*

≈

"It is delightful to enjoy and savor the sensitivity, skill and talent found in *Lungs of My Earth*; It stands out as unique, mind stopping, deeply expressive and resonates with my feelings for being in the sacred nature of everyday life."
—Dr. Alan R. Drengson, Emeritus Professor of Philosophy and Graduate Studies, University of Victoria

LUNGS

of my

EARTH

A Personal
Ecology

WILLIAM HENRY SEARLE

HIRAETH PRESS
DANVERS, MASSACHUSETTS

Cover painting: "Kingfisher," Amy-Alice
Cover and text design by Jason Kirkey

ISBN 978-0-9889430-6-3
Revised Edition 2015

Hiraeth Press books may be purchased for education, business or sale promotional use. For information, please write:

Special Markets
Hiraeth Press
P.O. Box 1442
Pawcatuck, CT 06379-1968

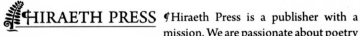 HIRAETH PRESS

DANVERS, MASSACHUSETTS
www.hiraethpress.com

❡ Hiraeth Press is a publisher with a mission. We are passionate about poetry as a means of returning the human voice to the chorus of the wild.

For earth

To encounter the sacred is to be alive to the deepest centre of human existence. Sacred places are the truest definitions of the earth. They stand for the earth immediately and forever; they are its flags and its shields. If you would know the earth for what it really is, learn it through its sacred places.

—N. SCOTT MOMADAY[1]

Don't let me leave before my eyes become sensitive and responsive to the life unfolding around me. Don't let me leave the life of this particular place that I now inhabit begins to enter into and take hold of me body and soul. Don't let *us* leave before the luminous world becomes woven into the centre of our consciousness, our concerns.

—DOUGLAS E. CHRISTIE[2]

CONTENTS

PREFACE

To us, each object is imbued with invisible fibres of light that reach out into the universe and are connected and related to all things and all times, and the song that the maker sang when making the object still hangs in the air.[1]

—ALEX JACOBS

Kumano Kodo, Northern Snowdonia, Barton-on-Sea, Keyhaven Marshes, The New Forest, and Hope Cottage: six places, six inter-locked spheres of light looping around my days; a luminous map of the sacred organised into a geometry entirely beyond the reach of intellection and yet within reach of that deeper, truer part of me which is also part of those spheres of light, those luminous places.

How have these places come to mean so much to me to the point that I couldn't live sanely without them? What is it, really, that they have given me towards which I cannot help but hold in high regard? What, in short, have they done to me to the extent that the tale must be told?

~

Kumano Kodo – that trail of pilgrims through the Kii Mountains of Japan, that trail that falls and rises, falls and rises through crowds of cedar laced in mists, crosses waters that ring over sleek stones as clear as a bell struck in a monastery at dawn, that trail that, after days of following its course, becomes a part of you, as vital as a lung. The trail that becomes the Way that takes you through places your soul has always known but which your little 'you' could only dream of. A kingdom of realisation ushering you on and on in further communion with the Way that governs and gives freedom to all things – has become a sphere of light.

Northern Snowdonia – with its wind-scoured rock, upright tombs of snow-bound granite, and raven-reflecting Lyns poised in the thunderous grace of the Cwms that echo with the creaking traces of the last Ice-age, the volcanic silence boiling in the heart of Moel Siabod, the Carneddau, Snowdon, and the cloud-shadows sweeping over the rough and high moors like the dark sleep of a god as it slides into oblivion, the script of the green and red lichens written by mountain scribes – has become a sphere of light.

Barton-on-Sea – the little beach and sea of my infancy, the speech and ride of waves lunging, lunging towards my dinky toes as I stood there as a vibrant and vulnerable child, surrounded by my family, listening to the waters that turned silt-skin brown in rain and jade-blue in sunlight, and moving the gulls with the wizardry of my eye into the sky's shell I kept by my bedside, and leaning upon the worn wooden timber groyne that was like the hourglass of timeless moments – has become a sphere of light.

Keyhaven Marshes – the wild aviary of wind-slung reeds and sheen of cracked mud where the curlew plods, the snipe wail and the kingfisher stitches turquoise ribbons over the lagoons that get ripped by the weakest breeze, and the egret lifts like an angel of white and silver air, the geese veering into the thick slough of mists that settle like spilt secrets around the bends of dunlin-haunted islands where cormorants dry their wings to a soundless music – has become a sphere of light.

The New Forest – those moist and messy woods of contemplation that delves amongst the roots in the fragrant haze of autumn, spying, through the thinning trees, creatures of the whole like I in my discipline, the dank shelter of rotten logs and tarpaulin roof shred by nails where I bask in a cold womb of self-erasure – has become a sphere of light.

Hope Cottage – a house of brick and mortar set back from a long road facing the wild heath, nestled at the trunks of Franchises wood, open to the sky and a horizon that tugs at your heart, a house open to outside, a house that lets the wind roll in and roll out, a house that shelters those desires to become integral to the earth, the desires of the contemplative, the end of desire and the releasement from the world – has become a sphere of light.

Taken together, these round landscapes of light, interlaced like the foliage of an oaken vision, provide the vital nourishment for a fresh and revived hierophanic taste of earthly existence.

Six places, with many places nestled within them, were prised open over time not through any conscious invasive effort but through a genuine desire to become unobtrusively connected to those places, connected in such a way that those places prised themselves apart under their own light and not under my shadow. This meant shedding, naturally first as in childhood, then through disciplined, discerning effort, that part of me which human society prides itself on perpetuating, the ego, the ability to stand back from the world of immediate experience and reflect upon it as though that world was so easily contained and laid out before us for our picking, the identity we are led to believe in as the most essential part of what makes us human, of what makes us unique and thereby removed from the natural world. For so long I had been living under a spell that seemed impossible to break through, the spell of the exclusive human crowned by the 'I.' Then to realize I had been living under a falsity was both unsettling and revealing. In that unsettlement I returned to the ground of my being, the ground being none other than the earth and the particular grounds of the earth where I could apprehend my most telling phases of personhood. Working to undo what had been done to me, to pick up the threads of the primal start of Being, was a searching for a light darkened by the human shadow, a light that still shines within and without, a quality of the earth as much as the air, the fire, and the water: an indefinable element that is the sacred.

Yes, the numinous must be earned. It's a gift rewarded through graft and craft of disciplined practices that cannot be taken away but only lightly held with an open hand, touched. If hastily clutched, the gift is spoiled and lost.

I have learned what these places have taught me, instructed me to do in the most natural way possible: to simply be and awaken to the numinous, sacred qualities of these places, these corners of the earth in which my renewed intimacy with the natural world was given the room, freedom and protection to thrive. But why, I ask myself, what is the relevance of all this, what does it really mean for me and the world of which I am a part that these places have evolved, through strict and close attention to their rhythms, to effervescent extensions of my own being and, indeed, of Being as a whole? To resanctify what is becoming increasingly desanctified, i.e. the earth, requires, first of all, a quiet rebellion on a personal level against the dominant modes of utilitarian action that are symptomatic of modern society. The first step, then, is to fall in love with where we are, where we find ourselves immediately and to learn to let where we are speak to us and move us beyond ourselves.

For most of us where we are now is not on top of a soaring peak or with our heads burrowed into a jet of mercurial water cascading down from the lip of a granite tower. No, where most of us are is less extravagant, much more ordinary: a street, a park, a winding lane. But it is through the ordinary, the commonplace, the overlooked, that the luminous heart of corporeal existence can be seen beating, albeit through an ashen veil that we have cast over it and turned the other the way. It's also about facing up to what we've done, facing the death we have caused, the loss of light we have accelerated with our darkness of being at once remote from the natural world and close enough to get what we want from it in terms of productivity.

Taking a cue from Thomas Berry, the natural world has been regarded as less a communion of subjects to be venerated and more of a stock of objects to be used as resource, fuel for the fire of the exclusively human society. The value of nature is not judged on whether how well it resists our needs to denigrate her into resource and inspires within us a riveting humility, no, it is judged on how well it complies with our plans of aggregation. Affirming

nature as a reductive means to the end of our expansive empires
has brought about the desanctification of nature. A sham sense of
the sacred prevails; the stone is sacred because it yields itself to us
without argument. Instead, the stone should be sacred because it
solicits our naiveté into wonder and companionship. Of this, Philip
Sherrard writes:

> By the phrase, "the desanctification of nature," I refer to that
> process whereby the spiritual significance and understand-
> ing of the created world has been virtually banished from our
> minds, and we have come to look upon things as though they
> possessed no sacred or numinous quality. It is a process which
> has accustomed us to regard the created world as composed of
> so many blind forces, essentially devoid of meaning, personal-
> ity and grace, which may be investigated, used, manipulated,
> and consumed for our own scientific or economic interest. In
> short, it has led us to see the world only as so much secularized
> or desacralized material, with the consequence that we have
> ruptured the organic links and spiritual equilibrium between
> man and nature.[2]

As the desanctification of nature *was* and *is* a process so too, I
believe, is its resanctification. Author of *The Idea of Wilderness*,
Max Oelschlaeger, was asked what the sacred meant for him and he
replied that 'it's the relinking, the rediscovery, the reconnection of
the little point of light, the sentience that you are, with the totality.'[3]
Sentience is the first gift that creation has bestowed upon us and is
the primary way back into the sensuous world.

Re-familiarising oneself with the body of a place and the bodies of which a specific place is composed can lead to a profound
sense of immersed belonging as a body into a carnal world. Only
at the level of personal and parochial experience can the process
of reversing the dark tide of the profane get underway. From this
reawakening and re-engagement of our animality into the animal
world, an event more mysterious may arise: the luminous quality
of that carnality.

Intense marriage to reality eventually, as I have confessed in this book of autobiographical spiritual renewal, can lead to the birth of a spiritual bond with reality. Arriving at a sense of God, or a nameless ineffability that suffuses the material world, is a natural consequence of that marriage. It is no accident then that I have used such terms as 'God,' or 'presence,' but, in truth, it is neither of these pale appellations. It has no term, it is beyond language and yet, this is what is miraculous, it is in reach of my sentience. The sentience that *I am first all*, before thought, utterly de-centers me from the moment, unravels every fibre and thought into the ever-shifting mesh of the whole that trembles with an electric surge at the merest influence and the merest rumour of thunder or birdwings buffeting the breeze down.

The six places within which both interrogations of sense-experience are documented and spiritual truths realised have been, for me, re-sacralized. But perhaps it is more truthful to say that they have *always* been abodes of the sacred. It is myself that has woken up from a coma of the profane. To use Douglas Christie's succinct description in relation to each geographical place that I have scrutinised, I have been 'a transformed soul in a landscape made luminous by his striving.'

In what follows, then, is a meagre and humble attempt to revive and evoke my own, personal sense of the sacred qualities of the earth by way of six prominent places that have served as distinctive junctures in my life so far. Situating this work in the context of what has become known as 'Spiritual Ecology,' I hope that this book may be accepted as an additional aid in the ongoing attempts, (made by thinkers, poets, philosophers, spiritualists, and even scientists) to re-awaken the brain-shattering sense that this earth is a perpetually urgent cause for reverence, awe, and kinship.

I

SELF-REALISATION ON THE
KUMANO KODO

More and more I realize mountain forests are good for
efforts in the way. / Sound of the valley brook enters the ears,
moonlight pierces the eyes. / Outside this, not one further
instant of thought.

—ZEN MASTER DOGEN[1]

Just as a white summer cloud, in harmony with heaven and
earth freely floats in the blue sky from horizon to horizon
following the breath of the atmosphere – in the same way
the pilgrim abandons himself to the breath of the greater life
that leads him beyond the farthest horizons to an aim which
is already present to him, though yet hidden from his sight.

—LAMA GOVINDA, *The Way of the White Clouds*[2]

I walked the Kumano Kodo, hastened there by an urgent need to
walk a pilgrimage route that seemed to offer a way into the deepest version of myself, a place that spoke to me due to its ancient
past and current practices of nature-worship. The very region
of Kumano in the southern mountains of Japan was and still is
regarded as a holy area of spiritual practices, practices based on
physical endurance and the body surrendering itself to the moun-

tains. I wanted to be a pilgrim for a little while, to become a minor part of the history of pilgrimages through Kumano, not as a Buddhist or other such label but simply as myself walking, discovering what Kumano had in store for me.

The trees were tall, the path narrow, waters clear and cool. For one week I lived one shrine at a time, gathering humility, patience, progressing towards a truth I had always felt homesick for. I wanted my footsteps to become as light as blossoms and my breath to become the breeze that barely sounded through the cedars, to dissolve and merge into the breath of the greater life. The blue sky shining between the highest branches I had ever seen was the purpose, no more than that, of my walk. I did not want to become more than the things I saw, heard, touched on the Kumano. I wanted to become them, I did not want to reach after something more because so far such reaching had brought about no lasting good. I entrusted myself to the path that would bring me no further than the simple abundance of the tall trees, the fragrant woods and birdsong that echoed to the moon. This way was the beginning and the end. Outside this, not one further instant of thought. After that, the Spirit would take over that which mere thought could not grasp. I released from 'I,' free to surrender to an unwavering obedience to the freedom of the Tao. Thus writes Lao-tzu:

> Before heaven and earth
> There was something nebulous
> Silent isolated
> Unchanging and alone
> Eternal
> The Mother of All Things
> I do not know its name
> I call it Tao[3]

DAY ONE

Off the bus at Takijiri I craned my neck up at the steep woods of the Kii Mountains and was taken in by a deep and silent green that smoked with an early morning mist. The bus crunched on the lay-by gravel as it U-turned and grumbled back over the iron and wood bridge, lurching away around the long bend of the narrow road, disappearing into the slow avalanche of mist that was curling and sweeping down, covering the bridge, the river, but not the river's sound; I held onto that sound in my ear as I adjusted my heavy pack and walked towards the beginning of the Kumano Kodo, listening to the river below and hearing my heavy heels clunk on the road.

Eager to walk off this heaviness that cloaked me I bought a bamboo staff from a small tanned man who couldn't stop bowing and stepped off the road onto the path made soft by a carpet of pine needles and crisp leaves. A stone-trough of clear water gurgling out from a bamboo pipe was full of faded copper coins, shimmering like sleeping bronze minnows. I washed my hands and paid my donation, bowed and turned towards the arch-shrine that loomed above me into the tree canopy. The path ran beneath it and veered up into the dense woods out from which thronged birdsong that I had never heard before. Here I was at the threshold of a journey. The mist thickened, this world was quiet. I walked beneath the great stone arch and entered the woods alone. At the first worn step I turned back towards the arch, gave a slight bow and looked up into the tall trees that seemed to rise higher the longer I gazed into their upright reach; shadowy towers in the mist that seemed to hold in the keep of their branches, secrets.

Steep sections of exposed, twisted roots and broken layers of stone made up the first leg of the walk. The day did not brighten but it warmed. A black butterfly painted with silver streaks was a distant fan falling and rising aloft on its own accord, jinking about my head then dancing a yard or so in front. It stayed with me for a while, this black butterfly like a paper-thin bird noiselessly heralding me onward along the path that, by a hot and foggy noon, swerved up onto a plateau, breaking up out of the trees and into cloud. At that point the butterfly fluttered away, prancing to and fro over the edge into nothingness. What did I feel here? What did I truly see? Habits of feeling, habits of sight. Thoughts drifted in to the moment and out to back home, other places. A deep breath focused my mind on the moment of mist, mountains, and trees, the Kii air, the larger life. This was why I was here: to see and feel anew, to be not what I think I am, or wish myself to be, but to only *be*. These mountain woods and its life would be the guides to that realisation. I entrusted myself to the power of Kumano.

> The way rises abruptly
> Into cedar mists,
> Strange birdsong,
> Water breaking here and there.

Arriving in Takahara for my first night's rest I sat upon a round rock with my back pressed against an old cedar, and looked out over the Kii Mountains whose tops were almost peering up through bulks of cloud. Down from the woods beside the first house an elderly lady, the first person I had seen all day, was bent low over her vegetable patch, rummaging and sifting through the soil. Frogs thrummed from the edge of rice-terraces that were neatly cut and set into the side of the mountain where the village dwellings petered out. I listened, with eyes closed, to the songs of the frogs and could feel, in that peace, the slightest of all breezes carefully dry the sweat upon my forearms and brow. Standing, taking a copper yen coin from my pocket and placing it gently into a small wooden casket that was used to prop up a weathered holy figure sheltered by a stone housing no bigger than a shoe-box, I then bowed three times, breathing out as I bent down, breathing in as I lifted, thinking upon my heart in this ancient place. Stepping backward down from the shrine and hauling up my bag, I made my way, bamboo staff in hand, down the long tarmac lane towards the inn. Swallows, countless many, darted and flicked in the air, diving and shooting a million ways, some alighted for a brief moment on the single sagging wire, looped around the few roofs of Takahara, then dropped, swooped in long arcs with the evening mountains looming up out the dark mist behind them.

I slept well that night, deep, and woke before dawn to meditate on the wood bench outside my room. I hummed the Heart Sutra as the frogs and cicadas hummed and thronged with me. I watched the mist rise and the mountains stand out green and big and ragged, a sea of them, catching the pale-gold and watery-rose dawn glow, but grey cloud cover descended in an hour or so, resuming the land with promises of rain.

> Frogs laugh in Takahara.
> Sickle-shadows glide
> Over water fields.
> Who is not thousands of years old?

~

DAY TWO

Soft, soft rain loosely fell through the tallest, straightest trees I had walked through so far. The narrow path of mossy stone followed the curve of the mountain, taking me deeper into the forest, further from Takahara. The mists thickened the higher I climbed, the rain thickened too, a pour of drizzle that cooled my body's sweat. I rested beside a still pond that reflected the green branches of the tree. A frog leapt from beneath the rock upon which I sat and crashed into the water, making ripples that fanned all the way across the pond, silently lapping against the banks. A swig of water from my bottle and I was walking again, keeping the bamboo staff in my right hand as I climbed higher into the mist and the silence. What secrets live here? What stories? I was making my own, part of the stories of pilgrims that walked this route through histories of self-discovery. The silence of the forest stopped me in my tracks. I had to take it in, the arresting silence that beckoned me on and yet did not let me go. What was it saying? The most fundamental part of me knew, knew in a manner beyond words, beyond thought, the pure listening of a deeper and more primal intelligence. The song of the saying was in the mist and the rain, a saying that is Kumano speaking.

> Rain on the Kumano Kodo
> Is a hundred bamboo staffs
> Clicking on path-stones.
> Who holds this one?

I resisted the temptation to wear my waterproofs. The rain-shower cooled the air and added peace to bare moments of walking and breathing, walking and breathing. The woods moved with me as I moved, stopped when I stopped, sat when I sat, but they did not daydream or think of other things beside here. That error of straying was on my part alone. But as soon as thoughts drifted they were tugged back to the moment by the Kumano forest and in that moment my thoughts were dissolved, erased. There was no need to think anymore, no need to dream of other places, things, people. All that I needed was here, the true gift found whilst simply walking to the beat of a heart and breath that was the beat of the bigger heart and breath of Kumano.

Now and again the same birdsong would thrill the air then die away into the mountain. Was it the same bird? Had she been following me, guiding me with her song? I listened to her as I walked, clambering up and over wet roots of the cedars that erupted here and there along the path like entrails, lithe and groping towards the rich midnight of the earth.

After hours of walking in the falling veils of rain and mist I arrived at Chikatsuyu, a village tucked between mountains, hidden from time. Hioki River, grey and shallow and wide, ran on through Chikatsuyu towards the Pacific, undergoing a pilgrimage of its own, in its own time. Down out of the green mountains that met to form a deep cleft, the river spilled and flushed onward down the wide valley floor.

Around the back of the Chikatsuyu shrine a buckled staircase led down to the river bank where I plonked my bag down and sat by the water looking back at the steep mountain woods where I had been immersed for the whole day. It was good to be out of the woods, to see the sky even though it was overcast, close, grey and raining. There was a large freshness about everything, even the round white stones smoothed by aeons of running water seemed new, only days old. Here, in this river, is where they said the pilgrims bathed to purify their soul for the next leg of the journey, to lighten their minds and hearts yet again, to gradually cleanse the caked on filth of self-delusion, egotism, that constricts every pore and nerve as they yearn to flourish and breathe in communion with all life. I imagined a warmer, brighter day for this but that's what imagination does: puts off here and now for elsewhere.

Make peace with me, the real, I feel the river say as it runs between my fingers and bulges up and around at my elbow as I submerge my right arm into the folded stream. Grey crystal, illuminated by the white stones that lined the bed, the water flurried up my arms as I waded out to the centre of the river. A biting wind kicked up from nowhere and riddled my flesh with a chill that was curbed only by dipping my whole body, slowly and patiently, into the water, burying my head in the cold depths, every part of me not truant from the immersion, the solitary baptism in Hioki River.

Breathless, taken aback, I vaulted back up out of the water, the wind clothing me in its cold clasp, and waded back to the bank to warm myself on the stones. I waited, shivering, for the profound renewal, the vital cleanse of my being. I looked back at the waters and at the green mountain forests and sensed a dim power that was beginning to show itself to me like the growing strength of a light, a sun emerging through old cloud. More of a deep feeling than a thought or a vision, that power subsided, the light gone again. The river had washed me clean to apprehend the presence of something great and necessary, the home of my soul that up until now was a mere pipe-dream. Is this how the pilgrims felt all those years ago? How did they thank the river? What did they see here in their soul's eye?

I said my vows, the Shi-Gu Sei-Gan, to the river, trying to let the water set the tone of the chant, its flow and timbre. As I spoke, my attention was taken from the water to a bird on the other side of the river nestled in deep, green grass. To make it out I stood tiptoe and peered, flushing it from its secret spot with the intrusion of my eyes. Big, heavy, gold-brown underwings striated with black lines, dark talons, its smooth sharp-beaked head tilted upward toward the sky, into the oncoming wind and rain. I was dwarfed by it, huge and gnarly, eagle-like with the hooked beak and precise eye, its feathers shimmering bright and sleek even though there was no sun to light him. I watched him and watched as he lifted, climbing the air in great oar-strokes and heaves of its wings until it found, to its relief, a thermal way up above me. Then, it drifted in one long straight line up, following the river back to the deep cleft in the green mountains, gone into the mist and rain without a trace, without a sound. He carried my vows upon his wings, my meagre 'self' struck dead in its talons; a sacrifice to Kumano.

> River eagle at Chikatsuyu.
> Empty village of quiet stone.
> Dripping water washes bitter
> dust from hardened cares.

≈

DAY THREE

Hot bright day, the mists, clouds and rain seemed like a dream that faded away with each waking second more in the mountain sun. The deep green slopes vividly glimmered, a crow shone like a black jewel as it tumbled down through the maze of cedars catching the rays of sun and the rays of shadow.

Three litres of water were packed. I was sweating in the shade an hour or so after dawn. There was a definite lightness to my step and I seemed to see and hear the things in the forest, on along the path, a little more clearly. Was that the effect of yesterday's cleansing? Did that eagle deliver me to the Spirit?

Miles of road walking from Chikatsuyu pounded my heel but by mid-morning a soft and constant breeze blew, which brought relief to the heat and my being. It was one of the most beautiful winds I had ever been touched by as it glided from the south and entered the mountain forests, releasing the dormant scents of the spring flowers whose colour and fragrances were lost in the darkness of the forest floor. Sweet wind, I breathed it in deeply, closing my eyes now and again to let the wavering light play about my closed eyes. The wind felt more like a light, or if the air itself became light, a blowing light some organ deep inside rejoiced to feel. There was a point in those moments of joy in the forest, wind and light when the road ran out to the narrow path that snaked up the mountain side. I could have stopped there forever cradled in that bliss with nothing more than the wind, light, the rustling cedars, and flash of crow feeding me, my most inner me. It was difficult to keep walking at those moments. Walking even at the slow and deliberate pace I was going was too much of a rush, but I learned to uncover that inner stillness so receptive to that world.

By noon the sun was at its strongest, its stinging heat felt between the protection of the trees. The path left the valley floor and wound steeply up, eventually bursting out of the tree line and into the dazzling blue sky that arced over and spread on forever at Iwagami Pass.

A dull yellow snake flecked with short lines of brown slithered into a perfect S and curled across the path then dropped down left into a low cover of thorn. Even though the view north was an awesome ocean of green mountain ridges lifted up into the wide heaven, I was glad to re-enter the cool dark of the woods with its fanning breeze whispering comfort through the shaking leaves of the cedars.

Taking rest at Waraji Pass, hanging my wet t-shirt on a branch that pointed up from the base of a squat and ancient tree, I took hesitant gulps of my water and lay back on the bare ground and stared up into the towering canopy, letting my eyes drift with the wind-swayed tops. With the deep earth holding me and the trees aiding my eyes into the infinite sky, everything seemed to come together in a single exultation of bliss. All the petty worries and anxieties of the smaller life one gets entangled in dropped away like dead leaves or rotten parts of a web and vanished, leaving this enormous welcoming space wherein I, not 'I' but more than I, floated as on a golden, boundless sea, rocked by waves of one-ness.

Such a spell did not last for long, broken by a pang of thirst for the dregs of warm water in my flask. I am not sure how long I laid there on that high circular clearing at Waraji Pass but time stopped and another kind of time took over, a time of expansion, a time wherein everything has time, given time, not the time that takes time away, that constricts.

> I am in these mountains.
> They find me, they lose me.
> The search is taking shape.
> A moving invisible cloud.

Leaving the Pass I headed clumsily down the rough path of root and broken stone that suddenly brought me out into a clearing as it levelled off at the mountain base to a clear river that brushed over smooth stones and slid on like a continuous pane of blue glass, smashing silently against the stones. I watched the shadows of a red and gold chequered butterfly dance on the surface of the turquoise stream. That grove was so quiet I could almost hear the butterfly's wings rasp against the air as I entered the cool arms of the water, stripped of all my clothes, naked to Kumano. To think that this river ran on down to the Pacific filled me with that excitement preserved only for thoughts and views of the vast oceans that fill this planet, and which break patiently upon unknown shores. As I bathed in the waters, every fibre of me surrendered to the gentle push, coax, and break of the water patterned with shadows and light. The image of this Kumano stream rolling on through wood after wood, reflecting the things it passed, shimmering and curving, then widening, meeting and blending into the other rivers, other streams—then all of them, all the water of the Kumano, as one moving on like the pilgrim's cloud, towards the Pacific, the sea, the destination of its wandering, became the picture of my inner journey.

Over a fallen trunk I sprawled myself, my legs and arms dangled down either side of the tree, lightly touching the fleeting brush of the water. Once I had cooled down enough and got my fill of stillness and silence of the heart, I stepped lightly out of the river, put on my clothes and kicked back up the bank and strolled onto the path. An oji-shrine, no bigger than my rucksack, was camouflaged amongst the undergrowth I patiently parted. Bowing, vowing, passing over a bright copper coin, I moved on gathering the healing power that each oji bestowed on me as I paid my dues, my puja.

With each small oji-shrine I passed, something, some burden hidden from my sight over the years fell from me and died amongst the leaves of the forest floor. Lightened with each shrine, the hours, moments became brighter, more real, more a part of being like the air, the pine-scented incense of the oxygen that exhaled from the million and one lips of the trembling leaves. In those moments the boundary between myself and Kumano faded away like a weak mist, leaving in its wake a clear and bright circle wherein all things were woven together by ribbons of light that danced to the silent music of the Universe that the Buddha smiled to hear. Was it me walking or was it the woods and light and wind, all one body walking towards the greater, boundless life that shines beyond every horizon, beyond every line of measurement the merely human eye tries to encompass it with? Where was I going, not the place-names on a map, but the destination that has no name, the soul's home, the Spirit's world?

> I am brought to Life
> By the sight and scent
> Of purple blossom whirling
> around Minashaku shrine.

By mid-afternoon, the dirt path widened into a broad stone that brought me, suddenly, out of the wood and onto a road that curved down around the mountain side towards my place of rest for the night, Yonumine via the grand Hongu Taisha shrine, all of which were hidden from my sight by the sloping walls of mountain woods. At the first bend in the road a strong wind blew, bursting up from the valley, colliding in the tree-tops, flushing a big raven from a branch. Flustered by the wind's rude awakening, the raven called three times in that stomach-deep way of theirs, tipped its bright black wings left to right and swished down the road, swerving up left and taking its perch on a branch that stuck out over the wooded ravine. Throwing its baggy bearded head and throat back as it called, another wind came rollicking up the ravine, shaking the raven's perch but this time, feet sunk tightly in the bark, it stood its ground and called again, three times, out of triumph. Wind and raven were at war, clamouring... but for what? Walking beneath the raven that paid no attention to me, I was reminded of the local Kumano legend of the three-legged raven, Yatagarasu, which guided Emperor Jimmu in his dream to establish Japan's first Imperial Court at Yamato. I would do nothing as grand and founding as that, but the idea that this raven may be a guide hooked me. He flew on, dipping and diving down the road, too quick for me to pursue. Would I see him again? Would he lead to my dream of breaking out of myself and into the boundless Sea of Being that glittered with numinous wave-crests?

> The three-legged crow
> Flies towards a three-fold moon.
> It is time to awaken
> From a two-fold world.

Passing through Fushigami village I watched a small boy run down the hill from his house to hold his mother while she dug at a rice terrace with an iron L-shaped tool. They were the first people I had seen all day and their actions, the boy and the mother, seemed a fluid part of the landscape, not at odds with it but quiet in their ways like the trees themselves that overarched the giant staircase of the rice-terraces. Late-afternoon sunlight paled to a ghostly gold hue giving off a heat that was on the brink of being lost to the cool of evening. A badger tottered towards me on the path immediately after leaving the tarmac road, quite happy and busy in its gait, then slunk stealthily into high, thick grass. I parted the grass with the end of my staff but saw no happy black and white figure glaring back at me. The path snaked through fields, rising to a ridge down which an ancient staircase led towards Hongu Taisha Temple, which was hidden from my sight by the dip and rise of the land. I took a moment on the quiet of the trail to bring myself back to the simple motion of my breathing, clearing the mind for the image of Hongu Shrine.

Not to think beyond what things most immediately affected me on the trail was my mantra, to abide with immediate things as they rise and fall through my senses was the means and end of my walk. It was through such obedience to the simplicity of the moments that pass as I walked I would enter into a fuller, richer, humbler order of being. This was, in fact, my most natural state but which, over the years, had been smothered out by those things, those petty things that seem important and urgent but, when compared to the simple profundity of the natural state (Buddha-nature), are nothing. To think, experience no more than what the raw moment dictates, became more and more important to me over the days and evenings of walking the Kumano. At that ridge gazing down towards Hongu in quiet awareness of the place, the air, my breathing, I knew – but could not put it into words – that I was edging towards a truth that would change the sense of who and what I am for good.

Eager to see the shrine, I paced on through the village and came to the high bank of the Kumano River, which was four-hundred yards or so in width. Heaps of slick grey stone lined the shores, trees brushed the surface, writing the leaves' names in the blue water in an inkless calligraphy. From the bank-top where I stood, looking down the valley, Hongu shrine loomed up in the distance like a mountain, dwarfing the few people that ambled in its shadow. Transfixed by its majesty I stood for a while admiring its shape, its beckoning grace daubed with the weakening, widen-

13

ing rays of the sun that was slipping behind the mountain skyline. A calm darkness suffused through the valley like the shadow of a mist exhaled from the mountains, blurring the columns of the shrine into a silhouette that rose up towards the first star like the gateway of a destiny.

> A blossom-shower of egrets
> drifts through Hongu Shrine.
> I am a wing of white petals
> As I bow, fold, then rise.

≈

DAY FOUR

I meditated in the dark before dawn at Yunomine in the moonlit cell of my ryokan. A full moon, distant and pinched, yellow-white and surrounded by her stars, was the point of my focus. Letting each part of me flow into her glow that filled the inn-room, the night sky, my eyes, with a ghostly light of peace my breathing became a part of the Spirit that circulates through every pore of Being, igniting the essence of every living thing.

> In the black heart of night
> Cicadas creep amongst stars.
> The ship-world's timbers creak.
> Kumano moon lights the Way.

I left the inn before breakfast and walked up the cool morning road to the temple where a service was being held. Invited in, I took my place quietly at the back, mouthing the Heart Sutra as the priest and the devout students chanted, filling the air, the mountains, Kumano itself with the pure sound one would expect to hear when true contentment takes over one's heart. Lasting thirty minutes, I thanked the priest, bowing as I walked backwards out of the temple, down around the burbling onsen whose heat scorched the windless air with a sour tang, then jogged back to the inn to attend a breakfast of onsen-porridge and raw fish laced with soy and lashings of green tea suspended in a delicate ceramic cup decorated with galloping horses and gnarled bonsai.

Black kites sailed in the hot air against a backdrop of sky that was as empty, vast, and wonderful as, I knew in my heart of hearts, was the very essence of myself. After three hours the path climbed steadily up out of the tall woods onto a plateau upon which stood a small oji-shrine, guiding the eyes out toward Kumano Sanzen Roppyaku Po, the 3,600 peaks of Kumano.

I reached Koguchi village by early afternoon, spending a while lazing in the clear blue waters of the river, toeing the rapids and floating in the deep baths of lagoons margined by mica-glinting rocks. As I floated on the swirling waters, letting the current turn my body like a mother's careful hand, mirroring the slow spin of the black kites as they wheeled higher and higher, the longer I stayed in that cocoon of stillness, the stillness itself expanded to become as vital as my own heart and blood. The stillness and silence became the critical fuel of my soul that was not my own property but an expression of the Spirit of Kumano, the boundless light that animates all life that this Way, this Pilgrimage, was leading further and further into.

The illusion, the mirage, of an individual 'I' tagged with a name became a palpable realisation, as palpable as the river soaking my limbs, as palpable as the warm wind that rippled the surface. What, then, is left when there is no I? Everything and nothing. Life becomes miraculous, even the most ordinary tasks become charged with significance that collapses the boundaries and barricades that one normally builds up between oneself, others, and the universe.

> The Way blows along.
> Who am I to say
> The wind does this,
> My breath does that?

≈

DAY FIVE

Pine needles, the curve of a single leaf budding into complete shape, the sunlight upon a tree, even the sound of my own feet scuffing up the steep and tiring steps of the Ogumotorigoe path came together in a single rhythm within which each thing had its right place and could flourish into the fullness of its being in concord with the rhythm within which it participated. Where was this rhythm, this harmony moving toward? Does it even have a goal? Why should it have a goal? Having a goal is a linear mode of thought made by the type of thinking that has to control the world. Such thinking I yearned to wash my hands of, to be purified, cleansed by this journey.

With each step I moved deeper into the moment, lending a strength, clarity and vividness to things as though a light shone upon them or, more accurately, from within them, blending with the sunlight. What was happening to me? With each step, too, I felt relief as though I were rising out of a darkness that had so long claimed me. Not exhausted but coming up for the true air of the spirit, I was renewed, revivified, reborn.

Criss-crossing streams, arcing around boulders layered in a velvet green that cushioned my palm as I leaned on them for support while I descended the rough path, occupied much of the day's walk interspersed with minutes of rest to glug on water, snack, and luxuriate in the ringing peace of the forest's golden bell. Two ravens, wing on wing tacked and swerved around the trees, their calls reverberated down the sloping mountainside. The ravens circled on down as the path skirted around the mountain, zig-zagging endlessly up to the tallest trees. I thought it was the sky I could see through the trees but it was the Pacific Ocean glimmering in the sun, huge and wild and without horizon. The Pacific stayed on my right as I stomped the path down the last of the steps into the environs of Nachi-San and its holy waterfall, Nachi-Taki, that bellowed and seethed even though it wasn't yet visible. The falls sounded like storm-waves crashing upon a shingle shore in the dead of night, filling the silence with thunder. After coming out of the trees into the open grass-fields that surrounded the village, I could see the massive broken line of water, frayed at its base like a rope whipping side to side, loosely tying heaven to the moorings of the earth. I couldn't take my eyes away from the falls, the grace and power of the water as it paused at the straight lip of the granite edge hundreds of meters up, then after a pause briefer than a heartbeat, falling breathlessly, attached to nothing but itself, utterly itself, falling through the hoop of time into the bright ring of eternity that splaying out, sprayed wide before the pool, fanning the brave trees that reached out to sup the water, clashing and striking the rocks and rolling onward through the deep pool towards the Pacific, below Nachi-San village. As I stood there in awe of the falls I could feel the water passionately sweep through me, haunt and possess my being. How could I leave this sight behind? Stirred and moved by the release of thousands of tonnes of falling water from the mountain forests, I sat upon a stone beneath a cedar until dusk as the stars flickered and the waning moon shone upon the white-gold, platinum-silver of the falls. That is what bliss sounds and looks like, I thought, that is what enlightenment is: absolute freedom from the illusions this 'I' builds up around the essential I, the real me that is a breath of the breathing Way, the Spirit, the Tao.

> Ryokan filled with half-light
> And the thunder of Nachi falls.
> How deep do I exist
> In the womb of pure Being?

I woke early after a black sleep and recited the Heart Sutra with my eyes fixed on a point of the falls, and with my ears on its sound mingling the sound of the Sutra channelled through my voice. After bowing to the world, packing my bag, grabbing my staff, I left the inn to catch the bus onward to Kii-Satsuura where I would catch the train to Osaka, then home. The falls thunder resounded in my ears, echoed through me even an hour or so after I had left Nachi-San and walked the final, pilgrim worn steps of the

Kumano, ending the path through the gateway of two enormous cedars stood side by side. I turned and bowed to the end of the path guarded by the century-old cedars that were known, locally, as 'husband and wife.'

I was not sad to leave Kumano. It did not want that from me. It wanted me to move on, leave the raft behind as the Buddha said, and realise what I had been through into my everyday life from thereon. How could I look back when there is so much to look forward to into the now? My whole way of seeing had shifted, but I was still tentative and unsure about whether I had gone through an awakening. Nonetheless, something vital was set in motion. That was Kumano's gift: inspiration, the breath of the greater life.

Sea-eagles hovered over the harbour waters of Kii-Satsurra, casting their great shadows on the surface. I watched them for half an hour or so in the dim, sea-fog light of noon, glide over the water then lift and take perch on a wire, then shriek across the town, gobbling their fish-prey caught neatly in their scissoring, spiked clench of talon. Save for the wailing eagles as they hunted over the harbour, the town was eerily quiet. A few people on bikes cycled down empty streets that were lined with closed shops and messy houses coloured only by lines and lines of laundry. Fishing boats bobbed and clacked, an old man sold octopus from a stall where they dried, flat and spread in rows in the muggy air. I walked out to the farthest point of the concrete jetty, looking back now and again at the distant profile of the Kumano Mountains, and looking forward between the cliff-stacks garlanded with windswept trees to the Pacific Ocean.

> Tapping of my footsteps and staff echo
> in the mountains long after leaving Kumano.
> A raven is building her nest
> Out of cherry blossom and light.

II

MOUNTAIN THOUGHTS

Here then may be lived a life of the senses so pure, so untouched by any mode of apprehension but their own, that the body may be said to think. Each sense heightened to its most exquisite awareness is in itself total experience. This is the innocence we have lost, living in one sense at a time to live all the way through.

—NAN SHEPHERD[1]

To lovers of the wild, these mountains are not a hundred miles away. Their spiritual power and the goodness of the sky make them near, as a circle of friends.

You cannot feel yourself out of doors; plain, sky, and mountains ray beauty which you feel. You bathe in these spirit-beams, turning round and round, as if warming at a camp-fire. Presently you lose consciousness of your own separate existence: you blend with the landscape, and become part and parcel of nature.

—JOHN MUIR[2]

28TH DEC 11
Only a god could explain how I feel about the earth. The roomy air into which the raven glides and rises, gliding again, upheld by a hand of the good wind is where I, too, have my silence. And the stars in a Snowdonia night are an anagram for the Word.

29ᵀᴴ Dec 11

There are words and touches in these rock-hard, southwest winds. Up on Y Garn the wind was so strong I could barely open my eyes and my ears seemed to cower in the rippling howl of invisible knives. Engulfed in mist, a million ghosts kiss-chasing ghosts, I stumbled low over a boulder-strewn summit, diving behind a wall of cairns to take a quiet, breathless rest. And beside me was a figure of light, shoulder to shoulder with me, whispering wonder into my ear.

30ᵀᴴ Dec 11

I walk the path slowly up to the lake that, on days like today, is swept flat by the wind. Or on some days, like yesterday, the lake is lost from sight in a cyclone of rain. Sunlight rarely fills the crags with gold; there are always clouds to overshadow that dream.

After moving to Snowdonia, I am learning to love cloud and rain, they give the light its unforgettable rarity, clarity. Indigo darkness fumes from inside high fissures down which white waters thrum, drape, and fade.

All my life I have wanted to be enclosed by mountains, to shoulder winds that make me feel heroic when I stand upright. It is like learning to walk all over again, crawling on hands and knees through heather, clutching loose rock that crumbles away through a helpless hand put forward like a weakened white flag of peace. Cold and braced, here I stand for the countless number of times.

Cwm Idwal. I say the place to myself even when I am not there, summoning it a little to keep myself focused on its moods and atmosphere.

Ravens swing in and out of Cwm Idwal's gorges like a child's night-time mobile. But I am not sent off to sleep. I am awake, and awakening. I am beginning to learn Cwm Idwal by heart but, like the heart, its rythms arise from depths only a god or a raven could plumb.

1ˢᵀ Jan 12

New Year's morning: I slightly raise the blinds and see an old man singing in a deep voice as he braces his right arm around a ram's throat as it tip-toes and slips on ice. As the only secret audience at the stadium of his sheepfold, it is hard to find reason to cheer. Pellet-hail dulls into soft shocks of a January dawn; a bird of black ice breaks loose croaking from the rock-hard wind. This time last year, I was in the warm woods of a southern district where a thousand trees wafted in the breath of horses.

Today, I have woken up inside the gut of Snowdonia where darkness can hardly lift above this cold world, where darkness is made by the sound of the old man singing a Welsh gospel of frost, by the sight of blood – a hot liquor – dribbling from the ram's slit throat, by a young boy waiting for the old man to take him to school, and by a dark bird flying toward a mountain clamped in a silent pain of snow where wounds of grass show through. The weather echoes through my bones.

2ND JAN 12

I watched a tall figure in the rain stride, and limp over Moel Siabod ahead of four dogs. He wore a thin black, unzipped anorak that snapped backward against the cold wind. He covered a great distance of knee-deep heather, bog, and rock in a short time, ceasing only once to peer across the Migneint moors, and to grasp the pack of sheepdogs around him. After pulling the small storm of his anorak over his sloping shoulders, then bracing his right arm above his eyes, lightly holding a barbed-wire fence with his left hand, he paced skyward into higher rain, and vanished.

The scene was almost two years ago when I was a mere holidaymaker to these parts. Why did it come back to me today? Since then, I scramble up Moel Siabod every day in all weather, knowing my way around her now even in night and snow. But I have never seen that strong, determined figure again.

Even though that figure was no more than a strong, fleeting ghost wandering over the mountain, he, more than any other person demonstrated to me the necessity to turn towards the mountains, the rivers, and winds and rain, to plunge my face into them and walk on, passionately intimate with the surroundings that well up through me like a fear. He has inspired me to be out there, to be a part of things, to share in the emergence and decay of life.

4ᵀᴴ JAN 12

Darkness down the Ogwen valley even though it was day, the northwest wind howling, after picking up speed upon the Irish Sea, and a world of rain following in its wake. I walked on, blindfolded by wind and rain. Rain dripped from my forehead and onto my lip. I tasted it even though I was not thirsty, not superficially so. But I am thirsty for what the rain speaks, the hallowed life where the god waits.

Reaching only as far as the one twisted oak, that broken, bent and twisted harp in an exposed valley, I sat beneath it, less for the shelter and more for the company. Putting my left hand around the moist and black hand of its low branches, which seemed to hold onto me in the storm, we – the oak and I – watched the squall of ferocious rain, wind, pelting hail and low clouds sail in shapes like gargantuan tribes of the giants and monsters that once dwelt in this mythological land.

I hid a pound coin in the sunken eye of its moss-browed bark and kissed its trunk, the taste and odour of earth luring me into depths of sensation I had never before known. The coin was a token for the ferryman who will take the oak onto the other side when all is ruined and no holy light can reach this man-wrecked world. I hope to see that oak if I am strong enough to endure this human storm.

6ᵀᴴ JAN 12

I trudged through ankle deep snow among high pines moving and seething in the wind. Sunset glowed over the distant, Glyderau plateau, and clouds made a pink and red roof over the valley, a glimpse of sky through the clouds, a window of chance for an emerging star. Peace. Still as possible. Listening to as much of the wind as I could, what my inner ear could permit me. I was at peace with something much larger but thoroughly integral to my own sense of self. Through being present to these moments in Snowdonia, I somehow become aware of a presence that thrills me to the bone. The most pressing issue in my life made itself known here – to be a part of nature. To feel it rush through me like a sweeping emotion, not to regard it as mere scenery. Snowdonia has taught me this.

7TH JAN 12

Ravens balanced the golden ingots of the sun upon the pans of their wings, measuring its ounces as the weight of one of my gasps, paying it out to the shapeless casts of the wind.

I love to describe these things and events. Focused description inscribes these images into my mind, branding them into my flesh. When I next step out of doors to meet the ravens, they will see that I have made the effort to include them in my life as porters of meaning. Focused description uncrumples the mind to include the dim life of the flesh in its vision of the world, and by including the body and the rocks and wind in its vision, the mind is unhinged from its human anchor. Description becomes revelation of what David Abram calls, 'a more-than-human-world.' Good poetry can achieve this, and philosophy should.

9TH JAN 12

Exciting performance of crows today in the winter light that shone, weakly, off of their dancing wings: an upland chase involving one gust of crows. Three fell away into the burning pit of day, two remained bound on the leash of the wind's torque spiralling into control. Air and each of them took turns to lead the chase. That bright unwinding of the grace of crows: passionate mascots of the coming night draped in kit of starry rain.

I ran my fingers through the rock's pelt of lichen. Mantis coloured, bursts of harlequin. The northeast wind was a million hypothermic ferrets among bare heather.

Out of the two remaining crows one broke free fueled by the adrenaline of sober hunger.

I urged them both onward beyond the drag of Clogwyn Mawr but one lagged back with a lack of boost, swung around and tumbled down. An airborne cinder kissed from a mountain fire. A black snowflake performing in the amphitheatre of the cwm. The others bee-lined toward Llyn Corin, becoming more famous in my life by the second.

Time and the crow let each other pass as she stooped, slipped deliberately through the fingers of the holy – the last grain of black sand in an upturned hourglass – to resume her rank among her fallen murder.

10TH JAN 12

Evocation of the presentness of a place requires a visionary stamina. A place of things ripen within the obedient gaze of attention so that attention seems to become native to the place itself, and eyes and ears grow out of the place where they have their roots:

Today was my first visit to the farm beside the lake. It sits on the top of a nameless knoll in the towering shadow of the Snowdon Horseshoe, with the Nantygwyrd River snaking around it like a dark moat.

Warfarin sachets were widely racked on shelves. Between them on hooks, hung blunt shears, clippers, and crooks. Ships of rain crashed against the barn that shrugged, wind got in through gaps, whipping heaped hay high into golden tornadoes that rose, fell, flurried down everywhere in volumes and flakes.

I was looking for someone, looking to buy a collie puppy. I have always wanted one. They were Land Rovers; a light was on, but no one was leering about. A black collie dog, thick-set sly, lay curled up on old coats, snarling as I passed. I gave him a wide berth that brought me into a room of tractor parts, ram-leg stumps, an echo of growls, and cages crammed with puppies yelping and clambering.

A raven hopped off, flew down from a rafter, almost brushing my head with his black wing, his feather almost snagged in my hair. I felt the cold pulse of his wing-beats upon my face as he merged like a shadow into the dark world outside, swiftly spun into a blur by the horizontal hands of the storm.

Waiting for a man whom I did not know in a place that was new to me, dizzying with the strong smell of use, I did not last long. The puppies quieted, the black dog shuffled like a weight of dust pushed through dust. Tin doors creaked on hinges turned a thousand times by people like me and not like me. Sharp hay whirled around in scattered crowns, voices of the indoor wind blew and wore. Out of doors, the rock farm track was a deep stream I could not ford without having to wade and swim.

12ᵀᴴ JAN 12

Do not get me wrong; I think the world of this darkness. Throats of the ravens of Clogwyn Mawr are wet with the bloodless dew of their calls. The gorge of Cwm Idwal, a nest where night sleeps as day cracks on, injecting sunlight into the mountain's veins of water. Strange men in the mists holding staffs flagged with skin flapping in the wind. The spiked rocks crowned with stars, and the moon upon which white creatures thrive and die as snow on the summits where I breathe so well.

How many times must I touch the river before a god shows itself? Give me a sign of the heart to let me know if I have loved this place enough.

14ᵀᴴ JAN 12

Outside light. The soul grows when its roots are in the earth. It suffocates, dies when its roots are in one's self.

A direct relation to nature is akin to godliness. A crown of mud, of sunlight, eyes immense as the sky, ears as wide as ocean-going winds, fossil feet, leaf hands, river heart on the rise. Breathing is easier than thought. Attend to reality with one's whole being. God is the shape of reality. Snowdonia is a part of that shifting shape.

17ᵀᴴ JAN 12

Thought must live and move among things, it must become a creature native to this place called Snowdonia. A stoat for example, slinking in and out of the ancient walls that necklace the throats of the hills, scurrying through the camouflage of the sea of heather far from the peregrine's daggering eye, is a secret of lithe flesh embedded in this landscape.

18ᵀᴴ JAN 12

In the mountains I feel closer to things, even at the summit. There is no end to how deep I can enter into relation with a particular thing in this landscape, this home. A boulder on the brink of the Crib Goch ridge is an inexhaustible world of sensory exploration. There is no need to travel to the end of the earth to 'find one's self.' One's self is here and now, it is that which I see, touch, hear, taste, scent. This 'self,' then, does not belong to me at all like some exclusive property. It is, rather, my humble abode. I reside within it just as the rocks and streams and clouds and trees do. This self is the boundless lung of the universe.

If there is an end to sensory exploration, then the end is myself. I am in the way. Thought, consciousness, misses so much. To admit one's profound smallness is wisdom.

20ᵀᴴ JAN 12

Hail clinks against an iron latch-gate. Sheep bow to buckets of winter feed. An owl pursues a stoat down a crag. Stars bud the tips of bare branches. The half-moon nests amongst pine tops. Twelve rivers bleed into one black lake. A cold wind blows across the road. Sleepless walkers like I wield head-torches at this unearthly hour as though to gather in the lost, finding nothing but a strange, frost-frail beam of thin light weaving to and fro as slowly as the growth of bone, that stops at each thing to stitch up each thing's heart, leaving behind traces of quiet that amount to the sound of everything breathing and working.

24ᵀᴴ JAN 12

Snow, egg-shell soft. The moon has been exploding all night, a shower of white ashes. A one-night blizzard, millions of white finger-tips tapping at the windows to come in, falling away into the night on the currents of the icy wind. In the morning, a white world with one raven. The swish and hush of its wings. I dared not step out of the house out of fear of blemishing the silent beauty with the deafening creak of my bones.

25TH JAN 12

Carneddau wind, plateau howl, crashing against my body, slipping around it, bearing the shape of my body into itself, carrying the cast of me away. I was imprinted into the wind, then forgotten, cherished, remembered . . . .

29TH JAN 12

Thought, reflection, should follow the curve of every mountain, the height of rock, the obscure depths of moorland rills, the clarity of granite born streams. Consciousness should take on the shape of the object that is perceived. The object is the mould into which consciousness is poured.

1ST FEB 12

Today I had the passionate feeling that the mountain was rearing up through me. I was the mountain walking, breathing, sweating. This disturbing feeling evolved as I walked further into its remoteness. Remoteness became belonging. Taking my first step onto the Siabod spur was the most meaningful step I have taken to this date. There is nothing more profound and mysterious than just being here. Here itself is everything. God *is* hereness.

5TH FEB 12

Afon Llugwy: nightly I go down and taste your waters, to feel the cold burning rush of your life in my veins. Oaks, whose textures I recognise in the dark, let go of the ghosts of their last leaves that float, spin in whirlpools as pyres lit by the moon's white flames.

A heron lifts, bouncing on the wind's wayward trampolines. When spring emerges a dipper will do jigs and twists on a bulb of rock. With my index finger, I circumnavigate a buoyant bug that hesitates in the spreading globes I create.

All I do is sit by the flow that thrives onward around the bend into a world I have yet to explore.

This one place is enough for now.

The river forever rehearses its sound, spawning improvisations of secrets where I will swim and listen to muffled thunderstorms from beneath the surface.

There are and will be no grand and fatal tales, no knowledge I invent and pretend to know, only this minor river, this mountain's daughter that seems so close it runs past the door of my home and by my bedside in my fondest dreams.

7TH FEB 12

Yesterday I was taught a wonderful lesson in wholeheartedness, commitment and devotion to a moment:

With one hand crimped around the ram's horn, the other hand clutching a wirey twist of neck wool, I wrestled to free the ram from a forked branch poked through and hooked around his horn. He was a heavy cloud of tired thunder. I had him locked between the weak vice of my knees to tame and subdue, firmly encouraging him to calmly steer forward so that the branch could slot back through, and fling away with its tear-drop shaped end to the sun. The branch was a black bone budging against his eye blinded with old and fresh blood.

Soft pads of gwynant grass were littered with skulls, sections of vixen, lambs, etc. I left the ram for some uncertain moments to go find help. A boulder wall covered in cascades of moss surrounded a cottage. The mountains of the Snowdon range behind the cottage were gone in a haze of mystery. Hanging baskets brimmed full with bits of bone, skeletons of flowers, clogged with ram skulls. The path up to the cottage door was well trodden by something that drags itself along the ground. I was in a commune of relics, fascinated by the lack of present life. But the ram! I ran back to him. He was rollicking, bucking so hard that with a sudden bolt of strength, the branch snapped free, and he hung his head down in astonishing relief. My hands did not hurt enough. He tottered off to gulp ferociously from a stream.

9TH FEB 12

I have repeated to myself time and time again like a mantra: there is nothing more profound than bare, simplest, sentient being. I will keep letting myself go until the whole of me runs out and fills with nature, and becomes, like Snowdonia, a part of the shape that is reality. Reality is God. I worship reality. There is nothing so deep as it.

10TH FEB 12

On occasions, my need to be out there among living things, moving among the bewildering stillness of rocks, the light bearing wings of ravens, the clear streams that move one to tears, reaches a kind of mania. I get stressed about not being out there. Inwardness is sickness. Imagination, a man's dreams, is a pale fever. I wonder when I am not out there I might have missed the one moment of revelation that will deliver me into the great truth I have always felt dimly flickering on the periphery of my being.

The earth is where we are soul, the soul's vital nourishment are the elements. Snowdonia has them all in overwhelming abundance.

12TH FEB 12

Wordsworth's 'One impulse from a vernal wood may teach you more about man than all the sages can . . . .'

I think I am starting to understand this. It will take lifetimes to fully understand it and live by it.

16TH FEB 12

Cloud blurred moon and the wind ransacking the one pine at the edge of the farmer's unkempt field. Tonight, the insane mare has ceased bucking, the mare that drives away, out of loneliness and for want of play, trespassers, walkers.

I hear the farmer scrub fox guts from his twelve year old son's hands after their lamping hunt without hounds.

I listen to a fly drowning in my bedside water, sucked into the vortex of its night-time reflection. Beside me, my fiancé sleeps. Her breathing could be anyone's breathing in this darkness. I want to protect the love I cannot see from God-knows-what lurks and gathers around our house in the dark:

The coal-man who grabbed and threw me into the road because I'm not local; a spider searching for its mate; the corpse of the violent drunk found in Bryn Engan, slumped sideways upon our garden chair. An ash-frail lamb languidly bleats in rain Chinook-thrumming against the rusty pen. The only good light there is the light coming at me from home (wherever that may be) upon the Christmassy-whisperings of the surf, the sounds of those who care treading unique and soft upon the sand.

I know this is sleep-talk, clap-trap, a nightmare indulgence. It will peter out in the shrunk ignition of dawn, and Snowdon, Clogwyn Mawr, the Carneddau, Cwm Idwal, will make me happy again, but for now, amidst these present shapes of fear, I want to go home (wherever that may be).

18ᵀᴴ FEB 12

Today, ravens, for whom playing is all, were held back by a fierce wind from joining in with the dance of the squall. The southwest wind, bred on the Atlantic, blew rain from my hands, which I pursed together to form a human bowl, to gather the transparency of the sea-bred, mountain-harried rain. But, in truth, I was hungry for the sun, the sun has been gone for days behind storms. Gutters rumble and growl. A birch tree, silver-white, collapsed like an old man across the road flooded by the Llugwy river. So there was nowhere to go except to remain in the fever of our new home where mould smiles down on us from the ceilings, the lick of damp chills our young bones into feeling rheumatic. And yet, arcing over Clogwyn Mawr, a rainbow appeared even though there was no sun, and it could, I thought, stay there for days, refuting my conviction that the god of light only travels in direct lines to the flowers of the heart.

21ˢᵀ FEB 12

First red kite in the open I have ever seen. I thought it was a buzzard planing over Cwm Penmachno, but as it sailed down in a great and elongated helix, I realised its forked-tail and its huge wing-span. Gliding down to a point in the air where it was visible to me it then began to float back up. It was a dishevelled prince riding up the valet of rain. Perhaps it thought that there was less rain down in the alley and feeling there was the same amount it returned on its spiralling staircase of air. Heron-like it flopped, tacked and veered. The bird was extremely effortless as though it were not gliding or flying at all. In one shade of light that was cast by a passing cut-out of cold cloud, its tail was a taut tongue of a strangled serpent trailed along in the talons of an eagle. In another shade as it rose higher, its tail was a split-in-two prayer flag hauled through the air in honour of the mountain gods.

I could not make up my mind about what he looked like, what he could be compared to. Shrinking in size as he ascended almost beyond human visibility, the long fingers of his wings pushed through the rain swept air like a child's open hand fanning through water. Something, some power, had a direct grasp of him as he sailed higher and higher, resting where rain could not reach and hit him in the face, but sunlight could find him, where he could catch the rabbit-prey of his breath while the doctoring windy light rushed to crowd around him, pressing its wide, voluminous ear against his heart – the windy light a stethoscope of itself, to listen for irregular breathing. Then a young god or spirit started to run along the ridge of the low mountain that enfolded the cwm, vaulting the bird high on a blue rope of clear sky that reeled endlessly out and there, beyond my sight, in a spell of clear weather, he became what he truly was and not what I thought or imagined he was.

Only when things are properly far from us do we see them for what they are.

22ND FEB 12

I know this raven: his home was the Douglas fir that lunged and swung in the wind, a shadow of wonderful omen clocking in-out in the rhythm of his day, moon and sun regular, a planetary- body that caught me, only to let go of me. Tugs of peace, not war. Now he's lying on his back with a broken neck in a rock-cobbled field of one horse. What does a dead raven look like in the eyes of a horse? I see what he is in mine: a black coal feathered in black ash, fallen from life's enormous, hand-shaped fire, fueled to burn more by his irresistible kindling of absence.

Life *does* remember him, and it's my human definition not to understand how, my littleness. I say it is indifference – those angels without minds of pity soaring above Clogwyn Mawr but it's really love, a kind of wild care, not violence. Other ravens, relatives perhaps, mob him to bone, showing his heart to maggots and buzzards haunting the world – ghosts of rancid flesh and blood.

The Douglas fir continues breathing honourably, lost of the raven's dark knot that twisted and untwisted itself toward the sky, crushed by sunlight, prised apart by a brighter light that's not of the human sun.

26TH FEB 12

I have managed to locate two selves that constitute my being, which occupy opposing views of existence. Snowdonia has, through my devotion to her, revealed this to me.

One self wants to rush, grab, break covenants of reciprocation. This self makes itself known when I am not focused on the moment wherein I find myself. I am only focused on my own orientation, my own world.

The other self desires to be still, to witness the awe-inspiring events of things *be*, to find pure joy in letting go, the rivers utterly flowing, the rocks being nothing but guardians of ancient silence, of experiencing the life of things following its own, mysterious course entirely out my control.

One self wants to dam, re-direct the flow towards itself. The other self wants to be attentive to the course of the flow, to perhaps now and again, when it's invited, step into the waters and wade through with open hands. There is no more profound experience I undergo than being a part of things being themselves, growing, flourishing naturally. What richness! And yet, I suppose, without the profane self that thrives on interruption and degradation, this other, blessed self wouldn't have become known.

The task for me, then, is to become more fully this blessed self. Or, more correctly, to let this blessed self become me. At present it is stunted. I must foster it with the wilds of Snowdonia. Every time I step out of doors and open my eyes to the miraculous song of beauty chanting around me, I feel that blessed self grow a little, and its growth cannot be gauged by the mathematics of human measurements. If it is unhindered, if it receives the nourishment of Snowdonia that it deserves, then it will grow and expand just as the universe is growing, expanding beyond the range of the net of our calculations. I have realised that there in no such thing as an 'inner man.' Interior landscapes are illusions that lead us astray from reality. They are landscapes within which we are lost. We must find ourselves out there, in the midst of rocks and ravens and ice. Resist the temptation to go in. Introspection is death of the soul, a dead-end. Must I stop this journal then? No, this journal is part of the process of self-amendment. I will stop writing when I am finally a part of the ineffable, unspeakable, life of things, when I take my place where the language spoken is silence.

28ᵀᴴ Feb 12

Beautiful walk today down the Nant Gwynant Valley, the sunlight homing in on great, wide rays from over the Moelwyns and shining upon the pines that roared above us in the wind blowing up the valley from Nantmor.

We heard Nant Gwynant goats tackle scree-steps high up on the southern banks of Y Lliwedd; their mountain-mulled odour was pungent in the cwm. We could smell them before we saw them. A bird, too quick to identify, kicked past through disarranged columns of pine, zig-zagging in a panic of doubt and loss. The moon-and-earth undersides of a buzzard were vivid against skeletal backdrops of poor, silver birches.

Entranced in the lowering fans of light that ushered in the shadow, my love and I, two young people, stood upon Elephant Rock, and looked out over Lyn Gwynant that shone clean bruising-blue in the gladdening triumph of a February sun.

Almost everyday up till today has been dominated by storms of rain, rain I never thought could be so powerful in locking me up indoors. There were no rain clouds, that oppression of grey-box air – only the prospect of being drawn further toward the pale fire of the sinking sun that glowed in the sky-hearth we were trying, trying to be warmed and uplifted by in the cold wind.

For all the emptiness that comes from not feeling at home here, there is richness; for how long I cannot tell.

1ST MARCH 12

I saw the shepherd's son, 'hearing things' today:

The shepherd's son was stood upon his father's humpbacked field, playing fetch with his new terrier that leapt up at him, yapping, and he laughed when it ran in circles around a dead tree. His father's collie couldn't take its eye off the doddery sheep, eager to bite at their blister-pustule heels. The shepherd's son urgently turned to face Clogwyn Mawr, that little scrubby rugged mountain, as though he had heard a strange, interesting sound. He just stood there for ages in an upright delirium as his terrier pestered the blind horse, looking up at the mountain, listening, while fine sunlight touched his eyes then withdrew leaving blank traces of infant gold in a face born old, and getting older. What did he hear that I did not? Perhaps, after years of being here, my ear, too, will turn its spiralling planet out towards the orbit of unknown sounds. Perhaps I will be able to hear the sound of the peregrine's eyelid as she blinks to clear away the blear before a kill.

2ND MARCH 12

Everything lives beyond the reach of everything else. And yet there is love.

Early, if not premature, spring Gathering: I went with the shepherd's son to gather in sheep from Clogwyn Mawr. Two collies ran in rings around us. A white glimmer, the dogs were off, sprinting into woods. One danced wide right into shadow, the other darted into scissoring light. We kept on climbing to the top, scrambling up the ridge of sharp massive rock. Lichens were luminescent scribbles in the sun.

The black cross of a raven swished into view, dangling its twig-legs down as though to grab prey, or land, but it dawdled, switching its head to and fro, then on a cold gust rode up into the blue immensity of the sky; a black star with clouds of torn moons sailed behind it. It was not only the flowers that were letting loose their gifts: the wind grew in strength, vividness, and from the summit I could see Snowdonia unfolding its mountains and valleys flowered with light, unleashing its contours and cwms.

Down below, the collies had all the sheep pouring through lowland bog – dirty milk deltas through paradise – hemmed together toward an iron cage where the shepherd's son stood watching, commanding, and his father whistled beside him, while I, the one not gathered, couldn't stop watching Snowdonia be released from winter by spring, and the raven, returned to ground, shook out tomb-hoary air, and loosened its grip on the rock.

3RD MARCH 12

3RD MARCH 12

Plunging my fists into the burning cold waters of the Afon Llugwy today suddenly took me back to my childhood when my brother and I would dunk our little fists into our grandmother's pond in winter. We would see who could hold their hands like that for the longest. My brother always won.

Today there is only myself to compete with, suffering the ferocious cold, watching the face of my reflection flinch, and my hand turn ghost-white, throb and ache like an open wound. But it still brought me joy to feel the river push and pour through my hand opened out like a fan. What human being is capable of such undivided attention as this river? I closed my eyes and the sunlight sparkling on the river seemed to sparkle upon the darkness of my closed eyes so that I was a part of the river, the cold, the darkness and the light. I was the river dreaming of itself, borne along, held, as though the river were my older brother, as though natural existence were a continuation of childhood. And to always remain a child, supported and upheld by the earth, trusting as to where life will take you, an unquestionable faith in the operations of the grand and tiny mystery that is life.

Contentment comes from being deeply in place, a place life has allocated for you, the primary place that is opened up for when you are born, not a place you strive to be allocated. We must allow the greater powers of life to move us into place. A child is unquestionably obedient, continuous even, with the current of life. My daily

visits to the Afon Llugwy instil within me this code of honour. The
river brings with it new revelations of knowledge. I have to make
sure that I am present. They can be missed in a flash, a fin-dive, a
bubble and eddy.

4TH MARCH 12

I would like to write about the nature of family, the mutual interac-
tion between the small community of family and the large community of the earth within which the family lives. There is a secret,
visceral story behind the reason for assigning family roles to natural
objects. Father Sun, Mother Earth, Brother River, Sister Moon, etc.
I feel I am almost at the brink of naming the earth as my family. I
cannot delude myself in thinking that I am wholly there yet. There
is still modernity to deal with, but my body is ancient kin. As long
as I am a body then my roots will always be in the earth. Humanity's
alleged 'homesickness' can be cured by the antidote of the body
that is forever healed by the swabs of grass, the wild wipes of wind,
the injections of sunlight that penetrate into blood and bone, the
alcohol of rain and rivers and seas.

5TH MARCH 12

As I leaned over the remains of a dead oak in the woods of Bryn
Engan the image of that figure in the rain, holding an axe at the helm
of a felled tree came to my mind and I wondered on it as much as I
would wonder on a creature that I had never seen before or heard
of. He was a big man by a dead oak in dark rain, wearing a broad wax
hat and a heavy foot-length coat that didn't swing around his ankles
in the strong wind. The axe was match-stick small in his hands as
he chopped wood, brushing four-bit split logs off the stump ledge
into sheep-beaten mud. There was a speed of sadness in his swing,
soundless, hunkered and clipped. He nodded slowly and steadily
at me as I passed in the amassing collapse of rain.

6TH MARCH 12

Clogwyn Mawr – a scrappy lump of grey rock and heather. Dwarf
mountain, belittled by the greater neighbouring sweeps of the

Carneddau, and the enormous bulk of Moel Siabod. But over time I have come to love Clogwyn Mawr more than any other of the jagged, arresting peaks of Snowdonia.

Today I made a new line of ascent. The east face, a scar of heather-shelves cut in by fat stitchings of sphagnum moss that squelched when I grabbed them, steep rocks that forced me to lean back, and gaze upward. Gripless, hands ripped to bits on wet thorn, slipping skins of luminous lichens, green and pale red and one raven soaring overhead like a black buzzard, croaking, gurgling the cool air.

I am familiar with Clogwyn Mawr and yet its charm of contact never fatigues, only brightens and buds. And the summit: a mangled platform of sheep-nibbled grass and rock slid out like half-risen prayer hands frozen in time. Clogwyn Mawr is a vantage point to view the possibilities for an ever deepening return into the landscape. Clogwyn Mawr offers up to me a view of home. Daunting, beautiful, a necessary walk.

And this is the hill, because of its subdued plainness unmarked on the maps, is avoided, unnoticed by crowds. But it is here, on Clogwyn Mawr, where the flow and shine begins.

8TH MARCH 12

The ritual of walking barefoot I adopted, natural after feeling more at ease in this wild place, was a mode of refreshing the soul. I soon realised that learning to walk barefoot again after decades of blindly consenting to the adult etiquette of wearing shoes – excessively protecting my feet from dirt and harm – wasn't going to be as pain-free as I first thought. For surely the skin on the soles of my feet wasn't aged-leather tough when I was a nipper climbing thorn-prickled crab-apple trees, trampling Mother's newly planted roses? Images of me as a barefooted, feral child let loose upon the world of the garden, or clambering over barnacle-studded rocks on the beach, skipping down tracks of flint, flashed across my mind, leading me to foolishly believe that if I could do it then, I could do it now. I was wrong.

The cold slabs of Welsh slate on the first morning of the ceremony were soaked cold by a night of northerly rain, making my feet burn and toes harden into digits of unfeeling numbness. But I endured the first test, clenching my fists as I ventured forth. I felt ungainly, like an infant on cumbersome stilts exploring a hostile world of new textures. The sun was too weak to leak out any comforting warmth as I entered a brave new world that didn't tally with the aboriginal dreaming of my childhood.

After the colossal hardships of adventuring across the slate, I abruptly entered the realm of grey asphalt; the asphalt drive that would eventually take me to the road, then after the road, the moist and moss-cushioned woods of Bryn Engan. The thought of the soft woodland floor compared to the sharp twinges of asphalt made me want to hurry, but to hurry, I thought again, was the primary reason why I felt disconnected from the good earth. So I slowed my pace, flinching, ensuring my whole foot spanned the ground, hobbling on towards my mossy and velvet woods of birch, pine, and oak, trying to be like Rainer Maria Rilke when he said:

> This is why I love taking long barefoot walks where
> I will not miss a grain of sand and will make available
> to my body the entire world in many shapes
> as sensations, as experience, as something to relate to.

The asphalt was like reflexology for the damned, stubbing and pinching on pressure-points, a minor torment in the cold morning of a slumbering, Snowdonia march. By the end of the asphalt, twenty metres or so of it, my feet were so numb it was like wearing shoes of ice viced and clamped around my poor, uncalloused feet. A couple walking their greyhound gave me a worried smile accompanied by an odd glance as I gingerly hobbled over the rough road, tip-toed over the wet steel cattle-grid, crossed the Llugwy bridge and made a bee-line for the woods.

Oak leaves from last autumn carpeted the ground like a torn and faded red carpet for the forgotten famous. I embraced the musty layer of leaves, avoided the tender tendrils of the melting frost, paying attention to every toe-press and heel-stamp, disciplining my awareness to the interchange between earth and foot, eavesdropping on their rustling conversation.

Folds and pads and pillows of moss eased my feet into a green submersion; a drowning alive. My feet, like hands, gripped the shallow root-work of still, bare pines that seethed in the northerly wind gusting in chilled fits down the Dyffryn Mymbr Valley. Soaked by the lathering moss, my feet were in their element. I could now relax away from the harsh tracks of man-made stone, striding up onto my favourite boulder that was wrapped in fleeces of coarse lichen and downy mosses squeezing out their wetness. Cushioned and standing high on the boulder, stretching my arms out to the tree-tops, letting my feet grip the rock, I became rooted in stone, moved into place. It was that simple.

The giddy thrill of feeling to be a part of the living woods was achieved by the simplest of acts, a discipline nonetheless. The blue morning sky glimpsed through the canopy aching to bud and burst into leaf, was as fresh as the crisp air swirling through my widening nostrils and down into widening lungs. And I felt that if I moved, the boulder, with its layers of dripping moss and undergarments of soil, would move with me. The sheer bliss I breathed in being a part of the dark and light world that swelled forth, didn't last long. I clambered off the boulder and made my way down to the black river to let the water gush around my feet. The water intimately explored every nook and fold of skin, and I slipped my feet out of the water and returned home.

Practising the ritual of walking barefoot every day through early, very early spring required dedication, particularly during the typical Snowdonia weather of gale-force winds, sideways rain, and diagonal winter blizzards. Now through every season I desired to walk barefoot out of the front door, across the slabs, down the asphalt drive, over the road, and into the womb of Bryn Engan. For surely, a full year of walking barefoot would prove to be a fruitful abandonment of accepted traditions, a quiet, meditative rebellion against the cast-iron mould my awareness is welded into, forced to ride the gaudy ferris-wheel of the modern craze of celebrating the forgotten kiss between earth and foot.

Walking barefoot was not only like a walking tree – enrooted, reaching up and out, breathing in and out the sky so that mind became blue and spacious – it was also walking with the *other* pair of hands: a handstand with my head simultaneously close to the soils and thrust into the air.

Subjectivity isn't only turned inside out in intercorporeal relations, it's also turned upside down. Now it's hard to resist not wearing shoes. Feeling a part of things, identifying one's self with beings, is beyond words and yet it is the strongest feeling that can be experienced, out of reach of intellection but entirely within reach of sentience.

9ᵀᴴ MARCH 12

Half an hour amble down to the Afon Llugwy – dark and quite shallow, deep where it is usually deep in the rain-fed and run-off troughs. Kept my eyes open as I threw hand-cups of water over my face; gasped, brief headache in the northerly wind coming up the valley toward the mountains bringing with it more thermals for the buzzards, gulls for the sea, ravens for the heights, gladness for me.

One swallow, first of the year, midnight blue-black, frantic, fatigued, jinking like a butterfly down river, wayward and tipsy. The weight of the Sahara on its mind. Then the dipper came darting, a continual thrust of giddiness, kingfisher-like but plump, a squashed fat arrow clicking, so accustomed to the river's plane and bending course. The swallow seemed to use the river like a blind man would use a stick to forage his way through woodland, inebriated with panic and indecision.

The dipper could see. He flew as though he knew where he wanted to go, desire met and fulfilled, focused, tunnel-vision toward the bulls-eye of rock that becomes his whole world to bob, jive, and twist upon. The river is his runway for take-off and landing, his destined and disembarking home. His flight does not tell of rehearsal and boredom. He seems genuinely excited as though what he is doing is for the first time. The swallow was much more adept in the spacious air, agile, in love with wide whereverness.

I looped back up around my favourite oak that was starting to show tales of early leafage, ancient and budding once again, then stepped over the moss-dribbled wall into the sanctuary of Bryn Engan.

Here is where I listen, here is where I am slow of breathing and soft of tread. New leaves, little green spades shovelling in the golden goodness of the sunlight, trembled. I wondered if the temperatures of their skins altered when I touched them. Bluebells – I knelt down to immerse myself in their scent, sweet but not sickly, fragrant, welcoming. My nose was the year's first bee trembling the pollen of contact. Patches of blue-sky raggedly woven through layers of thick cloud, clouds hardly moving. Distant dark plateau of the Carneddau. A great wall. Sun white-gold, soft-glow.

For an hour or half an hour I did not think, did not let thought steal the lime-light, the gorgeous gentle thunder of sensorial being. I was. The day has meaning now, foundation and a flowing heart of song.

10ᵀᴴ MARCH 12

What is my place in this world? I am a part of nature, a part of humanity, but apart from something or somewhere that forces me to question the solidity of my own ground and the fluidity of my perceptions. This missing place or thing, this blankness, makes me feel uncertain about the validity of everything, as though everything that comes before me on my way through this life were only temporary amusements, distractions from something quite magnificent, as if the world constructing itself before me was a mere carnival of thieves. This blankness is a black sleep going on outside of the arrangement of my self and which is the keeper of my greater heart.

This blankness needs to be shocked out of itself so that it yields its energy to the pull of the course of my life. Who knows what it may bring with it? It harbours amazing potential. A force released, a vital strength, driving the course of my life into an ever deepening unity with life itself. It hides the god of harmonies.

Or maybe, I have come to think, this space of nothing is a figment of my imagination, a fantastical hole. If this is so, then imagination, the culprit of illusion, needs to be dispensed with.

Attending to reality releases the whole pent-up potential of my being. The more I consciously participate in the sensuous world as it presents itself to me – there and then, point blank – the more I come in to my own. Rather than digging, rooting around for wholeness, I come to believe I must give in to wholeness, must give in to the gift of wholeness that is the peace of reality, the matriarch of belonging, the source of home. Reality is the source I must go back to. It is the death of being lead astray.

11ᵀᴴ MARCH 12

Today seven years ago, I first came to Snowdonia. It was those three days on my own here that planted the seed of need to come back here again and again.

Looking out across the Crib Goch, knife-bright ridge in the sharp angular sun-rays struck off the flanks of Moel Siabod, I am reminded of the time when I made an ascent of it. My first proper mountain.

I think it was a Saturday morning, thickest mist I had ever seen, thickets of wet, no wind. Snowdon is the highest mountain in these parts and the only Snowdonia mountain I had heard of. It was only natural to ascend it, the obvious choice.

With no real idea of the terrain, the weather, equipment I need to take with me, I took a bus to Pen-y-Pass that was deserted save for a few goats knocking antlers. In ripped khaki trousers, my brother's shower-proof jacket, brasher boots spilt and worn to slip-shod nubs, I made my way up the Pyg track. I can't remember much about how I felt or what thought crossed the path of my mind, but I remember the moment when I reached the point where the path forked either left or right up the steep ridge towards Crib Goch. I looked up at Crib Goch that was half-capped in swirling mists, black cliffs falling away like waves from the rising hull of a ship rearing up over me. That was my first experience of meeting a mountain in the flesh.

I tagged along with another man who was heading up to Snowdon via Crib Goch. Without him, I would've been utterly lost with no sense of where I was heading and how long it would take. The mist was so thick I could barely make him out three feet in front of me, a silhouette shuffling from aside to side, shuddering forward out of sight, then coming back into range, fading again like a ghost forbidden to enter back into earth and time, a man on the brink of losing it all.

Now when I traverse Crib Goch in clear weather I see what I would've come across: sheer vertical cliffs, towering pinnacles, labyrinths of rocks. Without him, that ghost guide (I didn't even ask for his name), I don't know what I would've done. I was a complete beginner, enthralled but foolish. Luckily that man whom I have never seen again – a dim friend always shrouded in mist – made the mountain accessible to me. I think it is not too dramatic to say that without him I would've fallen to my death or died of hypothermia.

Now, seven years later, the only way I can thank that man is to remember him as I look out towards Crib Goch, and find my own way through mountains. At times I think that he was a spirit of this place, still here, lingering. But it was better to remember him as real. I owe my life to him and to the living reality of which we both are a part.

III

SURGES

The sea's sound floods my veins,
above me the sun
grinds like a millstone,
the wind beats its full wings,
the world's axle throbs heavily,
I cannot hear my deepest breath,
and the sea grows calm to the sand's edge
and spreads deep inside me.

—ANGELOS SIKELIANOS[1]

I see its bright waves sweep across the dull and littered clay of my mind, and feel its surges gather, swell and roll through my veins that widen in these sensations of remembrance. It speaks to me – of what I cannot say, but I nonetheless listen.

Mountains and woods are new to me. The sea, on the other hand, is my eldest soul-parent.

≈

I saw the sea before I knew I had eyes to see it, and heard the waves – those big sounds of booming calm – before I could speak and shape the sea-air into words, that fresh tang of gales breathed into my nursery lungs. I gurgled like the frothed rivers of foam purling and swishing around the rock-bases replenishing the cloudy pools wherein time and my reflection slept amongst seaweed, roach, and green-crab.

My mother swaddled me in her salt-kissed arms that were as white and shimmering as the quartz-bands sewn into the rocks, introducing me like an offering of seeds to a visible god.

Before the prehensile, sluggish arachnid of self wove its abstract-ed web, its cemetery where the living buzz of the immediate hit of the world that is all too prone gets ensnared, dredged of its ichor and mummified by the vampyric 'I.' Before that leaching raid I was no I but an infant of the waves.

≈

A winter memory returns, an image enframed in frost that melts in the warmth of my rejuvenating attempts to remember it:

Once, as we strolled in the brisk night air on the cliff-top my father stopped to point at the stars above the sea. He began to name out loud popular constellations, passing over in silence those gold-en anomalies that seemed beyond naming and which, even now, I have no desire to know; my frail attempts to retain secrecy in a world of noise.

Seeming a huge dark column in the night with an outstretched arm, a gloved hand, and plumes of breath veiling those stars, he spoke in a voice that was the wave's ventriloquism. Mouthing, standing, breathing, imbued with a power, a still force that was not his own but the sea's and the night-sky's reply to his presence, I was enthralled into a magnetism that was not arresting but liberat-ing beyond any sense of freedom I have attempted to muster into comprehension since that stroll.

I cannot look at the stars without thinking of that mysterious night of instruction as though he were preparing me for this venture of re-discovering the dark heart of the sacred. Father, stars, sea, and I: a mythic night on the high edge, the cliff an altar, rearing up and out into an immense darkness that makes nerve-ends reel, tingle, and Being itch with an excitement of being touched by something quite wondrous.

I think that beyond what can be named, beyond the alphabetical summation of human experience, is a darkness that is dark because it is no colour I know. It was to that coloration of a spirit and to the accompanying dirge of the sea that my father was pointing to, or more accurately, what it was pointing my father towards.

Out of that darkness various shades of light emerged – toppling fragmented white-lines of peaked crests, glimmerings like *terra firma* stars running amok in love with recognition and contact, and chalk cliffs at the far end of the bay bearing themselves up like spires or icebergs of the moon. Out of that eerie creation the odd house window-light behind my father and I on the quiet road flickered into stasis like rituals of a community signalling rapport to the glistening of the stars.

What is this constellation of everything suspended in its own element? Why is it that the sea empowers me with a remembrance of a weightless planet of atonement that existed, exists, will exist?

That memory swelters into vision; then subsides into its frost-crypt guarded by winter as the sea, in my imagination, threatens to resurrect those memories in a tidal surge.

≈

Mother kept vigil on her pebble and sand shore of care – that little arc of Barton Beach – as Father, Brother, and I played amongst the summer waves like a family of seals.

First to take the plunge was the bravest and boldest, and first to spring up and dive into and through a curling wall of wave was the one we gasped in awe at – hero of the surf.

We would nervously undress on the shingle beside the wave-worn, wooden timber groyne and follow our broad-flippered father to the water's fizzing edge, forming a V like an arrow-head pointing in hunt toward its target of prey.

Our abandoned pile of clothes looked remarkable the further we inched away from them. The chill rose up through me like an inward and alien passion as I waded, gingerly, shoulder to shoulder with my older brother, past the knee and up to the heart gauge. By then Father was diving and chopping his flippers amongst the waves, rising up for air then arcing over the sun's sea-path of white-gold like the adult seal he was, breaching then re-submerging, breaching again, riding a toppled tumbling wave toward the beach where Mother smiled, clapped, and guarded our clothes from gulls.

Suddenly my brother would unlock from my intangible hitch and be gone into a world of wave, re-surface after the fallen crest through the deflated back of the wave sparkling, the taut blubber of his flesh shining in the sun, cleansed and cleanly invigorated. Then he would dash off swimming, splashing up geysers of spray toward where Father leapt up and dived down disappearing as though teasing a sub-aqua shoal of mackerel or other such prey.

I, on the other hand, was less confident with the switch in being, turned back between hesitant out-jumps of the waves' brimming surface-line to wave back at Mother who, more often than not, mirrored my wave.

Burning alive in the cold solution of salt and blood, the liquid struck a thousand matches up the flammable friction-paper of my skin. Soaked in the cold fuel of the water, there was no other option but to dive and douse myself out and away in the next wave, the most perfect and timely wave, hurling and building itself up layer upon layer until it loomed on all fours at head-height, birthing a shadow in its under-lip. Head to head we struck, a rutting between wave and I, and through the other side with precision and focus I thrashed awake more than ever to my surroundings – a vital exercise, a baptism of immanence, the wave a window I shattered through beyond my self.

All renewed, Father, Brother, and I, a family of seals twisting, turning belly up and down, crawling and floating in a suspension of human time, buoyant and aloft and at ease within the depth of becoming-other, becoming-seal we were. That was my first taste of the sea as an element of metamorphosis.

≈

I miss my kestrel, omen of my gallant childhood. She was always there, mid-air hoisted and faithful, on every occasion I returned to the cliff-top after an absence. She was a dancer frozen mid-dance, a lithe focal point of return effortlessly fixing me back into the bustle of the present moment.

Even now, when I stare at her in my mind's eye, she is a ballerina with beak and talons perfecting her display to the under-song of the inhuman world.

Steadily, and with extreme aplomb, she slid from being quite stationary, mesmerisingly so, into a fluid grain of intermingled thermals, angled into the wild air's salt-flecked grooves.

Where she flung to was where I headed. Between her and the sea was my catapulted way. Around the corrugated shelf of sediment cliff she swerved, herself the pilot and the plane, the draught issuing from her wings, disturbing the brittle cliff sand, planing past the bend into the open run of the small bay with her wings struck out as far as their furthest, hazel feather-tips could stretch.

Isotonic bursts, speeds of noiseless sound, adrenaline coursing through her muscle-twitch fibres, cells, nerves, her whole evolved, evolving biology; Barton's predatory athlete. And then, astonishingly, she would skid back round, tail fanned out, head flashed toward the sea's horizon, and unmove to a centre of nowhere.

I swear I could feel her heart thumping or hear it in my own breathing as I ran, stumbled, over wave-banked shingle, down and up steep, indented troughs of wet sand. Hanging above, hovering, materialising, her wings out like a welcome of indifference. I lay down beneath her on the warm stones with my arms stretched out. Would she stoop and tackle her talons and hook bullet-bill into the caged shrew of my heart?

Her maroon and sable-cream colours, her twitching eyes revolving the world in its visionary kaleidoscope of intensities I will never know. Her jerking neck, her very being *there*, were enthralling beyond comprehension, nothing less than ecstasy.

I fell under her spell time and time again, hypnotised by her alarming perfection. Crows and gulls mobbed her in a frantic aerial war to no effect. She held her own.

Changes, absences entered into my life and yet she persisted in a space of flying permanence entrusted to her by a mystery I dreamed she could see boiling beyond my feeble human sight, out there where the blot-pools of light spread across the distant prairies of water.

I miss my kestrel, her shadow careering and flapping across the cliff's pocked canvas, the crossbow structure of her poise and firing, her direct pitch of unimpeded intention, stamina and performance; the quintessence of concentrated being. I miss my kestrel. Home is where she is. She is earth's belonging.

≈

Cliff-jumping on summer evenings after the lowly claustrophobia of school. We were cliff-jumpers, my brother and I. I, literally, followed him to the end and over the edge into the blue nothingness, the giddy and frightening heaven.

The knack of gaining height was in the short run up to the crumbling, rabbit-burrow-weakened ledge. Then, the breathless leap, airborne neighbours of the gulls that eyed us side-on then swayed away, cackling and squawking. Weight and build returned in an instant's punch and down we plummeted, skydiving, kicking out our legs, rapidly rotating our arms, screaming. Then, the crash and tumble into the soft, rolling gold river-falls of sandstone.

Silence on that vertical desert, the hot sand embalmed our limbs in the avalanche. Buried alive. Gulls glided back at a lower level, seeming curious to what on earth we were. Birds? No. But birds we desired to be, to test our human limbs against the stomach churn of vertigo and the grab of gravity, the fleeting gift of grace as we freewheeled three-hundred feet up at eye-level with the sparkling horizon. What did the shore-bound people think? Fraternal suicide it must have seemed.

Where do we land from our heights now, my brother? I look at the steep cliffs now and they are eroded, weathered into rock-fall and slumpings of moist clay and barbed oak branches torn down from the top. The ledge, the runway from which we gained our youthful purchase, is gone into the jaws of the geographic time.

I wonder if there is somewhere now from which we can leap and can, on leaping, touch ground with a shock of jolt and surprise?

Perhaps I should re-invest those sensations of touching earth, of landing, in every step, every thought, word and movement and breath. The astonishment of being thrown along an invisible, incorporeal parabola and then, bang! The earth, the ground, the salt air, the sand and soil astonish me for merely being there to be upon and within. The silence, too, an aftermath of awe, allowing the room of awe to expand to be accepted into the shimmering environs of the local, parochial, and immense sea of earth.

Cliff-jumping was only a game – inconsequential play – and yet the images and sounds of it echo through me now as I blink and realise *where* and *that I am*. Brother, thank you, for that disciplining gymnastic of the truant soul.

≈

I loved to lay down in the wind-whipped winter sand of Shell Bay with my family. It was cold, and strangely warm. Combed back marram grass, those thick islands, green-gold and tall, seethed and soothed me to sleep where I lay in the delicate sandstorm that rifled amongst the grasses and hurried out towards the rending waves that fell like rolls of blue and grey steel, with my head propped up upon a salt-cracked and bleached log, or upon the warm fur of my dog. The sound of the sea poured into my darkest of sleeps that were deeper that any dreams, almost as deep as the sea itself.

≈

What is the role of retrospection in the endeavour towards rediscovering the sacred in the everyday? The gusto of poignant memories often acquires a limp when brought into contact with the clamouring insistence of the unpredictable present, but I have found that memory, rather than paling away into the obscure coma of an irretrievable past, is re-invigorated by occupying the same ring of light as the present.

A wave, for instance, is at once both a result of its onward propulsion and backward depth of support. It is an ancestry and offspring unto itself. It re-collects and releases the sea in a single surge. Re-collection, then, is a more definitive term to use when attempting to research and record the biography of the sacred that soon becomes autobiography, the sacred writing its own history through me; a compliant mouthpiece, a vector of sense.

My own past map of the sacred, if not aligned with the present, remains a mere relic. Through the eye of the needle that is re-collection, that map is woven into the ever-shifting un-mappable terrain of the present – not like a dead limb sewn back onto a living body or a faulty transplant of null organs rejected. No, it is more like a re-uniting of parent and child estranged by time then – this is time's paradox – fused by time.

These surges are vital exercises in re-collecting, gathering the stray parents of the past and bringing them home to the lost spontaneity of the present, constituting what Mary Oliver aptly termed, 'the family of things,' wherein I find my own self integral. What Thomas Berry calls the 'sacred depth of the individual' is also discovered through gathering together the communal, open family of things, the sacred depth of every other creature, wave, starling and lark. The sacred, regarded from this perspective of community (human and inhuman) is the blood of light that bonds the family of things together in a filial, historically evolving ecology.

≈

From the far tip of Shell Bay the bright chalk cliffs of Old Harry Rocks were too distant to warrant awe but, like the moon, they followed me and dilated, expanded and rose like eyes as I approached them with the shadow of myself. Running along the right were shallow trenches and knolls of sand dune wigged with ragged swathes of marram grass that rustled peace in the wind. Running along the left, the fledgling waves, nascent in the bay that was sheltered from the main blasts of the sea.

Our mother would take my brother and I, leaving home at dawn, to spend a morning thrill in the white light of Old Harry Rocks.

Baring their teeth, I did not find them threatening but inviting.

There, three of us, stood in the southwest wind that buffeted in random blows across the soft, green carpet of the cliff-top. Behind, the wild garlic wood was fragrant and pungent as gulls wheeled above us chattering, steering away down slanted tiers of air. Shags and cormorants, one after another in a train of flight, stayed low over unbroken waves and beat over the sea towards the next bay, or further out. I looked at them until they flew out of sight and tried to breath in time with their wing-beats, their controlled commotion. Their wings beat up and down too quickly and I panted like our dog who skidded, sniffed about elsewhere on the sloping down in his world of instinct and delight.

My brother and I stood tip-toe, trying to stroke the breast or wings of a gull, the under-wind ruffling their feathers as they pointed their yellow-painted bills that dried in the sun. What did we look like in their eyes? What were we? What affect did we, two children, have on their trajectory in the world? How did we fit into their lives? I know how they fit into mine. And the cormorants too, those submarine angels of the sea.

Down over the overhanging edge we peered. Our mother let us lie down and inch our eyes over the lip of grass and see the waves claw and pick at the base. She stood over us, behind us. Her strawberry-blonde hair curled over her face in the wind.

The longer we looked, the more the sea seemed to rise up and clasp us; the cliffs seemed to dwindle and aggregate in size at the same time like those racking dreams in which everything moves away and into our innermost bone simultaneously. Losing our focus and bearings, the sea was only an inch away like looking through blurred binoculars. The waves were thunderous in our eyes. The wind wanted us down, down, there with it in the whirlpool. The lobbed salt-spray tightened my skin. The earth wobbled beneath us as though undergoing minor fractures of displacement and earth-quakes. Was our mother conjuring all this wonder? Was she capable of carnal wizardry, of putting us under 'the spell of the sensuous'?

Aeons of clouds sailed over us, casting shadows in long strides over sloping Ballard Down. If we fell, there was no doubt we would've drowned, tumbled down hundreds of feet to a messy death. But those fears did not enter us. Those fears were nothing in a place of joy were we felt secure, safe. And we welcomed the long sleep home in the warm car.

≈

How can I expect to hear a god before I've been spoken to by the earth?

≈

Natterjack stream fretted down through the clumped and crowded little wood hanging at the far end of Chewton Bunny. That dark and dirty stream, brown and black with silt and soil, too dark to mirror my smiling face, splashed down from a rock-ledge at the wood's end and flushed towards the sea that spewed it out.

Chewton Bunny: a miniature valley, my childhood kingdom dene in which I was king, the birds and hedges and grasses and sand my people, my followers. I led the stream with hip-high staff in hand in its brief exodus into a pool where it rested, collected itself into calm before disappearing beneath risen ramps of shingle, then re-appeared into the sea. The vanishing of Natterjack was magic to me. My brother and I would often attempt to dig down to find the waters, but to no avail. The shingle's secret: I respect that now.

The kestrel often hung there above the sacred stream. My father swears he once saw her bathing in the pool. Stonechats, too, abounded in the sparse woods that covered the model-size valley.

With their spearhead wings tucked in: the stonechats, clacking, flicked themselves from catapulting bramble tips, bulleting and bobbing over a slumped sand cliff-divide, in sharp arcs shaped to the curvature of the sun. Their plump shadows badly photographed by the Natterjack stream below were dear to me as they paused on runaway air to switch direction back over the two steep sides.

The flocks must have been stuck in a broken record of flight or else they were busy perfecting, rehearsing it. Four, no, five times they repeated the voluptuous stunt of volleying themselves back and forth from cliff to cliff. Their pollen and gnat flecked bodies beat like hearts bleeding their colours of flint-white, bruise-blush gold, as they rested in brambles from their tense adventure; being but the child-pitched pebbles they were and are meant to be.

If there is one place I should pick out as a place in terms of the quality of hierophany it would be there, Chewton Bunny. Not spectacular but a wonderfully mundane geography shaped by weather and sea I was most familiar with. A funnel for the southwest winds and a haven for quiet and silence during restful days.

I was astoundingly innocent, ever at the ready to be cast. It was the primal place of my childhood that lit up my inner receptivity not only to the physical world but the inkling of the numinous life that I felt surrounded the Natterjack stream, the stonechats, and the sound of the sea at the valley's close.

≈

I close my eyes and see her, that strongly postured cormorant, standing upright and alone upon the red painted, stalk of steel sticking up through sea and thrust into the light.

She eclipses the sun as she dries her broad and ancient wings as though embracing, like I, the vision of light, sea, and sky. Her wings tremble like thick black silks of laundry in the breath of a beautiful, revenant giant. When she lets her dried wings float and fall down to her sides, with her head raised and looking out in a manner of receiving an anointment or blessing, she diminishes into a dark and faint outline, a silhouette, the sunlight blazing out and around her form as though she herself were emerging, solidifying from the sun, filling out a predetermined form that's already present and waiting like a container to be filled.

Waves lap and crash gently around the seaweed coated top of half-submerged rocks. Even though she is as black as a raven at night she seems a creature very much of the light that nourishes even the stones in their skull-hard skins into fully-fledged beings of communion.

I remain looking at her for a long time in my mind's focused eye. Like the kestrel, she effuses within me a powerful sensation of return, settlement, and homecoming. Gulls glinting like white emeralds veer around her in an orbit of declaration. Alone, stock-still upon the steel spike far at the junction of a million and one tides and secret mackerel shoals and cold currents lacing through hoops of warmth, further out than I could swim as a child when I splashed amongst the waves, is she resting? Is she 'thinking?' Is she staring? What does the world feel like to her as she stands out there surrounded by sea?

Imparting wonder into me by merely being what she is in the only way she knows and will ever know, not deviating from the destined song of her course, absolutely herself with an air of confidence I can only dream to inhale, a figure as fundamental to me as my own heart. We know, I feel in my bones, of each other's bare and simple existence.

The emotional connection that echoes between us does not fall into the short-sighted categories of human emotion, it is something within which I am bathed and in which the cormorant is bathed. We are not one, no, for if we were one I would not be aware of the delightful rebellion of her remoteness, her own identity towards which I am first of all pulled. It is only by being intensely and persistently different that – and this is the irreducible mystery I cannot, nor would want, to get over – that we are drawn together by within a web by the work of the web itself, the industrious and liberating whole.

I desire to see her more and more herself out there, beyond my miserly, grubby snatch of understanding, above the calm sea of blue and glittering light, and then across that extreme difference of identity do I feel, I am, most intimately a part of *our* existence.

When I am dragged far from the world of palpable things I close my eyes and picture her out there in the light, surrounded by deep seas on all sides, and I am brought, gradually in slow and sure exhalations and inhalations of breath, back into the wild home of things.

≈

I lay awake at night hours after my father carried me to bed and my mother kissed me three times on my forehead then firmly tucked in the duvet with her fists around my sides and the base of my feet. Leaving the bedroom door four inches open on their graceful exit to allow in the hallway light – a reminder of indoor life in the house-quiet of the night – to fall in across the carpet and rise up in a diagonal strip along the dark-blue blinds, I said goodnight, to myself in the gathering silence, to my family, my dog, Ollie: an amen at the end of that animal prayer.

As the quiet began to waken – the idea of a 'dead of night,' was and still is nonsense to me – I could hear, building around the edge of the planet my ear turned on its axis toward the prevailing wind blowing outside, the sound of waves crashing slowly onto the shingle beach and feel, too, the greater silence that belongs to the night-sky above the sea between the stars and the quiet of deep, near and distant oceans.

In the moment of hearing, the bricks of the house-walls became transmitters of sound, shells, open windows through which my hearing and the silences met and rolled into one motion like a wave moving forward. I read in Coleridge: 'The one Life within us and abroad/ that meets all motion and becomes its soul!' Often I think upon that now, that celebratory remark of insight into the commonwealth of being, as I think back to that quiet of oceanic night.

Then, if mists lay in swathes and ribbons of torn and fissured cloud upon the sea, the lighthouse, perched upon the ragged hull of the Needles, thrummed and revolved its night-light, guiding ships from iceberg rocks into a clear passage down the Solent Pass towards docks where derricks and men waited on the harbour wall.

The lighthouse light, a night-light like the hallway light in my room, was followed by two blasts every twenty seconds, eight or so waves, fifteen snores from my father and brother, twenty odd beats of my own heart. I listened to the horn as though to a master-voice singing like a good siren in the darkness and smiled myself down into a warm sleep, my bones and bones of the house tremulous with the reverberations of the waves and drone, and even, too the sea-mist floating around the house to steal it away, encroaching upon me like sleep itself, the bringer of forgotten dreams.

Gulls on the tile roof were my morning alarm. Rocked and washed clean by the sea, I tasted salt upon my lip and could feel the walls of the house, through my palm, contract into brick in the mild kiln of day.

~

The night-fishermen's fires were a line of stars fallen amongst the rocks. Thin fires clicked and snapped amongst the tons of rock. Dark figures with glowing faces rose, perhaps once or twice, in the space of an hour to kick the fire, sending up a flurry of sparks to the heavens.

I walked down the path to see them. Blood and fish stained their baggy sleeves and reels. Too timid to ask if they had caught a fish, I merely lingered amongst them. Some times, if I got close enough, I could see their broad chests swell up and down almost in time with the night-waves that fell upon the shore invisible like the after-life of a dream. The mood was one of calm, of laze, and ease.

Imagining three fat bream below the surface circle the unfurled flags of bait that drifted upon swapping currents, the lead weight like a tear scraping and dragging through dark sand and seaweed, a pendulum that doesn't quite swing all the way back because of the counter-force of the pulsing tide, I wanted the fish not to fall prey to the rod's trickery.

To the blinking tankers upon the Solent horizon and trawler-men ranking up wet-rust winches, the fishermen must have looked like a constellation of the shore, or flare's run-aground or Chinese lanterns burning brightly and caught on a washed-up lobster-pot. I wondered what they thought of out there where I will probably never go.

Nocturnal gulls floated silently by, eager for scraps, rich pickings, like torn off laces of white rag, or brilliant ideas of white in the conundrum of the dark.

≈

As a child growing up by the sea, I had a recurring vision to become expansive, to be an infant of the sand, orphan of the sea, a phantom of foam.

With a stranger's footprint upon my heart, a paw-print upon my wrist, a gannet's feather lodged behind my oyster shell ears, I wanted to be *of* the sea, a mythic animal, legendary. When I spoke I wanted my tongue to clack and speak a sound that volleyed forth an explosion of stillness, whisper in surges, roar in pools of engulfing calm.

Gulls would be my angels that attacked me for my dreams of periwinkle dark, for fish guts entangled in the net of my soul. I would thicken into clumps of rain, my eyes little purple jellyfish throbbing to be borne along the waves to nowhere in particular.

Silver in moonlight, golden in the sun, I would wander the same beach over and over again like a hermit or lunatic of the shore, beaten together by the ocean's hands into a fine, smooth specimen of driftwood that would burn blue and bright and sizzle hotly in any home fire no matter how decrepit. I would be indispensable to anyone's wonder. If I was invited to build sandcastles with other children I would be the sand, the ground-up shells, the dead green crab enrolled as the king of the fort.

A figure of natural bliss, explored by the fingertips of the expanse of sky and the sea, the very earth would find me fascinating as though it couldn't believe that I was born from it. I would certainly have wings, old and as athletic as the southwest gusts, like a cormorant's; sharp, stiff, and honed but albatross big. With one beat of my black and huge wings I would be able to circumnavigate the bay and, catching a glimpse of myself, in the water, I would see a holy profile, deep and moving. My moods would be off the human scale.

≈

One day I was a cold child quickly undressing on a golden arc of beach, shouting my first words at herring gulls aerially warring with surf, raucous and grating on my nerves. I was, with my brother and dog, a sand-castle king, a summoner of storms binging on ice cream. I remember how we used Father's flip-flop as a spatula to flip pancakes of foam into the air that our boisterous dog barked at and bounced up to snap his teeth at. Off-white snow, tacky on the skin. Mother didn't like it when we asked if we could take bags of foam home. And do what with it?

I kissed stones; I still do now, lobbed and skimmed them like prayers across the water. The ripples fanned out like laughter.

Then, in the course of my consciousness playing and growing to the instructive song of the sea, I was struck by the thought of lightning spangling the sea, sizzling fish, shocking congers that swayed deeply and morbidly in the broken cages of sunken wrecks. I thought of them, often, the congers, those long grey snakes waiting for me.

Hunkered down like a misty owl between rocks, after school before tea, I patted the rock's quartz skin as though they were scuffed bellies of best friends, chums. With sticks of driftwood I drummed a tribal beat on my little blue bucket. A native of an unremarkable place, a place that looked like an abandoned quarry in the rain. My life was a life of light on shells; my history of desire has been minute as salt-grains in the immense sky.

Awkward adolescence arrived on the scene. Waddling down Fisherman's Walk like a daddy longlegs on stilts, see-sawing drunk with the fatigue of not knowing what I was, bulbous with acne sores, the sea was my soothing stability. The wind went nagging from crow to gull, striking my kestrel in a whisked and whistling globe of air.

Swimming alone whilst my dear dog, Ollie, watched me from the shore, was my healing. Seaweed and stars were my dressings, my bandages. The timber-groyne was my ancient seat, my throne.

Today, I am a man still thinking of the sea with the same quiet and devoted passion. For those who are close to me, expect that I will scribble my will into the sand with a crab-claw.

≈

To begin, continually, with *that* I am: the discovery of my – or the – endeavour.

≈

A wide feeling of spaciousness opens out in the act of attentive stillness, watchfulness, towards the unfolding and re-folding of the waves. Expansive without being dislocating, the sensation of stillness that arises from meditating with open eyes and ears upon the sea, from being as still as this body I am can be – not in a manner of self-arrest, but in a style of restful staying within the motion of the moment – becomes as concrete and strong as the sea itself.

Adrift without visibly moving from a trough of shingle, engaged in an attentive homage to the waves and distant quiet of blue, the world of the sea becomes more full, more present. Ripening, blossoming under my obedient gaze, the sea becomes an extension of the blood that courses through me, the rocks become extensions of the bones that support my posture. I become less present to my own personal existence, my own limited awareness of myself and am taken in, accommodated, by the blue, the white, the golden song of sunlight, music in the flesh, into a collection in which 'I' like a piece of drift-wood is cast up upon the shore of its own reluctance.

Lagged back by its own limits of mutual participation, the 'I' disintegrates into a solution of blood, sky, and sea in which this moment *is*. Where am I now? What is this that moves me further out into peace and also further into the undertow of the world? I am born under, thrown under and emerge: *sub-ject*.

Even as a child staring out to sea on the nearest beach to home with Ollie, faithful at my side, those feelings of boundless stillness and joyous belonging in the centre of Being, were palpable then as they are now. Maturity, in terms of years, has not diminished them, nor the past of immaturity belittled their real impact. Sat on the shingle with my knees to chest, my left arm locked around my shins, my right arm wrapped around the warm back of Ollie, staring vacantly out to sea, I was as old as the sea itself, and as young.

Then the profound stillness and silence would pass like the end-roll of a soft, one-off sea breeze, and I would return to the earth-enware of myself in the same regular pattern as breathing in time with the ebb and surge of the waves. Hardened back into the seat of shingle, withdrawing, blown away as it were, from the liquidity of self and sea – the immediate world of ice-cold stones, mid-morning sun, the shore running waves, captives and liberators of their own power, the thick worn wooden groyne, the warm fur of Ollie bristling beneath my hand, the shape-shifting clouds caught in their own currents the highest gulls are enamoured by, the shadow of a turnstone as she flips stones with untiring diligence – took on and still takes on a renewed vividness and heightened palpability.

Down by the sea, Being breathes. My child-lungs, chest, and body were small, frail, but my breathing was huge and capacious.

I hear now the sound of the waves in my own breathing as I sit here thinking upon what the sea has given me and what part it has played in my life and in my pursuit of the sacred in the everyday, the overlooked, the gleaming ordinary.

≈

On a big-wave day after school, I remember my brother and I standing in our wet-suits on the cliff ledge in the wind. With our cheap boards tucked beneath our arms, beneath clouds building and interlocking like joints seeping into one another a marrow of bruised darkness, the colour of almost-rain, we leapt down the cliff and ran in a race to the beach. He was always quicker than I. The waves were huge. We looked across at each other with a kind of geeky tension in our eyes.

Ankle deep, we edged in a foot at a time until up to our necks, the chill water spilling in down the gaps around our necks, we jumped abreast onto the board. Committed, we swam out. The rain fell. The waves rose. My brother, older though he was, clutched my ankle in fear. The waves kept wanting to push us over to the rocks so we had to keep swimming hard against them towards the bigger waves. Now, the cliffs behind us were distant kerbs of sand. The only way back was to catch a wave, to swim would have been disaster. Waves, like white ceramic lions, rose and roared and crashed. Whirlpools spun like gigantic potter's wheels in the sea's rapid and burly hands. The sky darkened into the onset colours of dusk.

Sand martins flitted above us, little kamikazes. The weather and waves (the waves had their own weather) seemed strong enough to tear those little birds apart, but they were gone in a flash back toward their nest, their cliff-side cubbyholes.

The waves were too big to ride. One held us under for at least a minute. But you held on the whole time down there to my slim ankle. Our boards were snatched away, broken to pieces upon the rocks that seemed so close we could see them, as we surfaced for panicked chances of air, face to face. I thought we were gong to die. A lump of timber, car-long, bobbed by. It could have struck either one of us on the head. I didn't want to see my brother's blood that afternoon. Every time we tried to kick and thrash out of the pits between waves we were sucked further in until, by sheer miracle, one wave lifted us up together like the way our father used to and propelled us toward the shore. All I remember is being lifted and then the pain of sharp shingle upon my belly as I was hurled face first onto the stones and crawled beyond the wave's reach. My brother had somehow reached the safety of the shore before me and he was sat cross-legged staring out to sea. Rain came down in diagonal lashes like a thousand soft whips, and the waves hated us, except one hero amongst them. Out there at the wrong time, my brother's eyes seemed to say, is a world of panic. We were like two washed up creatures, dazed by events that could've led to one of us, or both of us, not being here today.

Since then, I greet the sea with respect. There are places where we should never go.

≈

Waves chop themselves up in the moonlight. Their crests, like white serrated blades, hack into other crests and mica-spray spouts up in plumes like fountains of moonlight. Waves arrive from all directions out of the windless dark, bow, buck, jolt, and slam into one another in a rut. Antlered, the crests ride up and subside as though sizing each other up; animals of the ocean, a species unto their own. In one undergoing roll the waves collide and power forward to me where I stand on the shore in awe at the games of water. Then the single wave as long as the beach itself, a round black bar chequered in sparkling moonlight, pauses, stops. The one unbroken pipe of wave then unrolls itself out and upward like a cloaked lord without a face. Rising over me, the wave stands. I approach, not frightened, and touch the black body of water with my outstretched hand. I press my ear up to it and hear its moonlight-heart beating, and feel its lungs expand and contract, expand and contract. What is this beast?

Such are the dreams I would frequently have when circumstances found me far from the sea of my childhood. Even now, as though it were real as day, I remember the cool flesh of the water on my palm as I stood there before the beast of waves. Other dreams followed. One where the sea rose to the cliff-ledge, and one where waves towered so high they crashed into the clouds, one where the water would clutch my ankles and drag me down into its depth wherein I swam down deep and deeper toward a strengthening fissure of light, a crack in the sea-floor full of the most golden light that was always out of reach.

In my dreams the sea was an enormous presence, a primeval force like the thought of the universe itself as I live out my narrow cavern of a profane life that hearkens toward the sacred.

Of the many dead or dying creatures I found on the beach near home it was the dying guillemot that has stuck in my mind the most. Feather-scattered gulls, Peregrine-blasted gulls, rotten crows, and washed up dogfish, no, none of them has laid to rest more heavily on my mind that when I failed to help the guillemot:

I regret that it was winter. Pulling my coat around me as I traipsed over the shingle, throwing a stick for Ollie onto the bleached line where sea met sand. New Year's Day gulls teased the fuming crests that toppled harshly and cold onto tin and iron rocks. Heftier stone frost-skins mirrored the dull ill ache of the sun, the sun that was the sky's slipped disc in the cold weather that made the world seem arthritic and painfully slow in its spin in space. Halfway along the beach, passed the timber groyne I happened to find, at my feet, a young guillemot laying straddled in a mess of fishing-net twine. At first I leaned down to inspect her closely. She was frightened so I stepped back and approached her from a more secretive direction. She was on the verge of letting the frayed twine entirely claim her. Any energy she did have was almost certainly spent struggling to free herself. My dog, noticing her began to bark but being aware and obedient, he backed away with a single swipe of my hand as I stared at the bird. Kneeling, I began to unpick two knots of twine that were roughly snagged in her feathers right down to the vane. Not taking long I stuffed the net into my pocket and removed my coat to lay it over her in protecting darkness. Once covered, she stopped twitching. Unable to resist the temptation to take a peek at her, I lifted the sleeve of her cover and looked into her eye that seemed to pierce, blankly, beyond me or through me; I couldn't make up my mind. What was I to her? What did my alarming presence feel like? There was a mesmerising vacancy about her eyes, prehistoric and yet fascinating.

Her bill was a flint arrow of charcoal, sharp and black. Her eyes made contact with mine and the communication was unutterable. I didn't know what to feel. Caked in tanker oil, gyrating her black-glue embroiled wings, twitching her paddle feet, I gently and carefully place the sleeve back over her tender head. I then carried her up the beach away from the sea towards the wooden beach huts where I thought I could keep her safe around the back, out of the way from prying eyes. As it was my first experience of handling such a beautiful and injured creature, I thought it best that I pass her over into more experienced hands. After ringing the Royal Society for the Protection of Birds and being assured that they would take her into care I left her, stupidly, where I presumed she was safest.

When I look back now I realise that I panicked, left her stranded, prone to wave and crow. I abandoned her.

65

The next day, after a night of a full moon encircled by three phantom rings of bronze and platinum dust, and the sea flinching at my window that shivered in the wind, and unable to stop thinking of her down on the beach, I found her, dead, nestled into needle sand. I looked at her for a long time, knowing I should have done more to help her, bearing the cold I should've bore.

≈

Ynys Llanddwyn, that tidal island of cormorants, black rocks and winds that beckon one like the promises of solitude. On my first visit there, gale-force winds hoisted the sea into waves that dashed head-first on black rocks, their shore-bound dreams of Malltreath Bay shattered into white blood spilling over and around the block of pillowed lava that define that pre-human haven of Anglesey.

Blear hail-sheets billowed over the Menai Straits, fork lightning flashed and sprang above Snowdonia. I could not see into the far west through my squint eyes toward the ship of Ireland that was hidden behind folding, winter waves, waves of winter. Moved to shelter in a small bay of shells and clumpy sand, almost out of the wind and flicked by rain and the rain from waves, I kneeled.

Whilst I knelt there in a refuge of quiet, down from an island of pinnacled rock, in a little tidal pool, a grey seal breached belly up rotund, sleek and sheen, rolling, yelling like a child for attention, huffing and puffing, lounging upon the upright rocks. Then, from underneath a ceiling of kelp, a seal pup coyly rose to the surface, all eyes and whiskers, fins and fat, buoyant as a watertight bag of white-flowers, playful and bemused. For an hour or more I watched them swim beneath a crowd of cormorants huddled wing-to-wing, quaking and hunchbacked as they nervously preened.

Like a weak friend coming to from the point of sliding backward down a steep verge of total, coma dark, the sun emerged, feebly reaching, touching my shoulder with its golden fingers. I swiftly turned and showed my face to the sun, and smiled in a salt and fresh showering of sea rain. Distant blue holes slowly widened above the

Irish Sea, troughing in the crib-rocking storm hands of the wind criss-crossed by busy bulleting cormorants.

Six wild, white mares strayed from St. Dwynwen's holy ruin of whispers, their long manes yanked down by the wind as they pressed their mouths firmly down onto grass tilled by hermits long, long ago. The old lighthouse shone as though washed clean. The quartz roods, lichen-flecked, shimmered divine signallings. I stood there amongst it all, rapt in trying to hold ground upon an outcrop of rock, my arms splayed out either side of me in the gentle on-slaughts of fading rain and light: a religious figure frozen in time, in a riot of outward awe.

Do not let me forget that day, that place almost gone to an early tide of night, the black petal-soft cormorants falling off the black flowers of rock, the seal and her pup, those roaring breathless moments heard, only dimly now as though through a shell, in my mind of minds and heart of hearts.

≈

Today I returned to Hurst Spit; that length of shingle stuck out into the tidal hell of the narrowest Solent Pass. Five miles right down the coast, my parents house, my childhood home, crept nearer to the cliff ledge that has been eroding by meters every year.

Tennyson Down, where my mother took me, and I saw the peregrine eye to eye as it emerged out the sea-mist, and caught my gaze. And Old Harry Rocks far off to the west and visible, palpably so, thrummed in my heart like an inward shock of bygone days never to be recovered. Between the Needles and Old Harry, the open sea where the sun climbed high on its ladder to share its lamp with my soul. Grateful to grow up there, I knelt, chose a stone, kissed it and threw into the waves.

Stepping up onto the flat top of the banked shingle, the wind struck me and the scent of the sea cleansed my nostril, my perceptions were cleansed and I saw, in a vigorous instant of humility, that everything is holy. I was happy.

≈

At Barton with my mother, I watched one gull, beaten astray from her flock, that swung around the pivotal bait of the sun and struck the southwest wind. Blown back a fraction-length of a feather-tip, a clean body of compact glittering sea-foam, she steered forward tilting and threshing like a maddened scythe manoeuvring through acres of resistant white, then she dipped down straight, locating an aim that was no figment of direction but real, decisive expansion of a golden cyan way that rolled away beneath a heaving, sunlit sky. Then she floated, cast in a flame of calm, toward the strong forearm of Tennyson Down or Old Harry Rocks (I couldn't tell in that moment) her compass being so much more detailed and exact than mine, that was wrapped in a jesse of numinous blue.

I think that the fury and the joy of a spiritual presence beyond names, more than God, was in those wings, in the streaming vaporous light, the broad wind, the shadows and the waves, the deepest and shallowest swirling currents, the hidden channels, and in all the bright, high creatures that have been airborne, flung from the holy falconer's arm, and in the ones that are standing by to be born, called forth, blessed then released across the sea.

≈

We can have inhuman parents, parents of the earth that nourish us, parents that have lived before our own and will outlive them.

I know that the sea is an alien element. All humans are weak swimmers in her domain. I could drown in her and die, and creatures die and thrive within her around the clock. But the truth of earth's vital biology does not mitigate its mystery. The sea surrounds my days with a luminous energy that takes me beyond the dualities of life and death. Her rhythms and sounds are my soul's home.

IV

ECHOING MARSH

Being, not doing, is my first joy.
—THEODORE ROETHKE[1]

Creatures of light, creatures of light.
—TED HUGHES[2]

Throttling herself upward into the blue span of the sky, the sky like a blue hand reeling her up on a sparkling thread – I think of the petite motor of her heart and imagine it swapped for mine – the skylark, jittering, sings of the bird's eye view, sings for all of the birds here that are not as steady in perspective as she. She trembles under the weight of transferring every other bird's vision into those black and barbed-grain eyes of hers. The song she sings is the song of every being alive with vision. In the completeness of ecstasy she rises into the palm of the sky and vanishes. The whole day sees and sings, sees and sings.

≈

Entering the marshes as quietly as I can through the smooth gate that, if I am not mindful of taking it slowly, swings back and claps shut into the clunking latch, I sidle down the bank of tall grasses and hide in the reeds that seethe along the border of the first lagoon.

It is a quest of mine not to blunder into this place, beginning first of all with how I open the gate. Opening and closing the gate that

69

seems to mark a boundary between worlds of gradations of light, is a test in the quality of my quietude and how far I can develop myself into an unobtrusive being. It is an exercise in passing into this world of thin reed, bright water, and bird, discreetly with the motion of care. More often than I would have preferred, I have thoughtlessly allowed the gate to swing back on its stiff spring-hinge and slam, all too much like a gunshot, into the post-clasp. Every bird after that blunder is flushed from their secrecy where they safely abide like jewels of precious anonymity and the travelling V's of Canada geese disband, scatter and call.

All because of one wrong sound, a sound not consonant with the purity of this place and a young man lost in a momentary blur of ill attentiveness and thoughtlessness, the sacred space is invaded, disrupted, and pallored. From then on, after that percussive error, all I see and hear is already lost. I lag behind the frightened beauty of things and view only the fleeting shadows of their flight.

My right desire is, as Simone Weil puts it:

> To see a landscape as it is when I am not there . . .
> When I am in any place, I disturb
> the silence of heaven and earth
> by my breathing and the beating of my heart.[3]

The sense of myself as a disturbance is most prominent here amidst the throng of marshland. It's not that I shouldn't be here it's that I should be here under a different name, a different guise. There is a place for me in the orchestra of Being, I know it, but what I also know in equal measure is that I'm living in the wrong key. The salt marshes are my place for the advent of attunement through the practice of myself as less of an outside disturbance and more of an inner, effaced, natural addition or accompaniment.

≈

The principal features of Normandy Lagoon: roughly thirty acres of shallow water, border, and stripped spreads of dwarfed and angled

heather; a small wood of bramble, gorse, and sessile oak; the stag-
nant sluice belt smeared with a putrid skin of algae and other bad
bloomings but speckled with sea-pink as though they counteract
the stench with sight of fragrance; enclosure of wire-fencing; a long
and flat grass island in the middle of the lagoon; curves of white
sand here and there; pools dotted amongst the winding land; no
reed-beds to hear the high wind through, the reeds sigh at the next
lagoon. And then there are the birds, the fretful choirs of this place,
robed in a thousand colours, antidotes to myopia.

For a place, such as these marshes, to become a sacred place or,
more accurately, for a sense of the sanctity of a place to become as
manifest and as concrete as one's own sense of hearing and sight,
requires discipline of attention. This process was not known to me
when I first came here through the gate of bliss and stepped onto
the sea-wall that runs for a mere five miles from Lymington River
to Keyhaven Harbour.

It was in the throes of stumbling adolescence that I first came
here, and I had no idea what would be in store for me the more
I returned here and faced its music. Of course I took note of the
surroundings, the Solent whapping to my left against the jigsaw arrangement of the steep, ballast sea-wall, and of the off-shore islands
reigned by a squabbling mob of gulls, and the quill-tipped reeds
writing their invisible and momentary autographs in the air – but
that was it, I merely took *note*.

Following the route of the sea-wall at a constant pace takes no
more than an hour and a half to reach the end-gate at Keyhaven.
Three hours, then, to the gate and back, in the undecided stance
of adolescence, in a state of potential being akin to the Aboriginal
Alcheringa, wherein all things have yet to be fully formed and because of that are still underway, living and singing with no termina-
tion of creation in sight. Back then in that awkward state between
boyhood and manhood hooked on a tame visionary endeavour in a
gentle landscape, I ask: was I moved by what I heard and saw? Did

I live up to what lived up around me? Was it mere scenery unable to break through the barricade of self-consciousness that builds itself up around the person that wall's him off from the 'harm' of luminous otherness? I know now that what had to be done was to chip away at and wear out that wall of inner defence cemented with pride for that vibrant place of reeds and birds and sea-birds to escape into me and for me to escape into its whoosh of presence. There I might become a majestic continuation of Life within which I am also bound, wound and unravelled beyond myself to the very last point on the farthest thread of myself and there, teetering, I could soar.

It wasn't too long before I was hooked on the place and would return most days and nights to show my face to waters and the lapwings and snipes and stars. I also knew that I could be more hooked, more taken in by everything, more attracted by the turn of the wind's phrase in the complex sentence of life, like a sound played upon the edge of every stray thought that wasn't drawn in by the moods of the marshland and the moods of the elements amongst the moods of the birds. I bombarded that place with the hope of being shown something quite extraordinary. In a time of my life when I need to be chasing other things I was chasing something else here, something else entirely.

≈

Lapwings tumble across the sky in the dark, seeming of the dark themselves and yet illuminated by the torch of the ground.

They corkscrew down in a single hitched carriage, brush their bellies over grass, drift high on wings paddling, reaching, and straining into passing currents of air, boring forward with a bounce over reeds that whisper rumours to neighbouring reeds, haunting the heron that stays still in fear, cloud-light and sliding over sand chequered by their shadows painted by the moon.

They are calming to remember and to look at – those porcelain messengers of earthy light, spreading the word of themselves amongst the well-read earth, bleating across the mud-flats – and to breath in time with the image of their lit flight over sunlit or moonlit marsh: a dazzling covenant between here and I, shaken by a wish of wind as the lapwings declare something glorious as they spiral, one after another, lapping the sky and descend amongst the mild nests of stars that wait for them upon the ground.

≈

Normandy Lagoon is where the main haunt of the lapwings reside. Pockets of them drift down towards the creek scarred mud-flats like snowfall at Keyhaven and settle in the smaller lagoons. In most instances of drift, they flap back after brief touch-down in clouds to Normandy Lagoon where I, sat amongst the spiked-gorse in the warm hair of grass upon a head of mud, wait for them.

The lapwings on the ground nearest to me do not notice that others of their kind are arriving in delicate storm clouds. Will there be enough room for them? The sky is roomy enough but it is a dream to suppose they could live in the room of the sky until their lives are done.

I could watch lapwings for the rest of my life. They fall towards each other like white leaves with surety, and softness, and weight that only becomes apparent the closer they get to one another. They bulk out and solidify under proximity. Until then, they verge on weightlessness and ripe anorexia of Being. Gravity and grace are at work within them. The fallen tumble down amongst the already fallen and flutter their wings in stringent greeting, pause, then shyly close their wings to luxuriate in their hereness.

November ushers in billowing clouds of them, hundreds of lapwings lapping the still cold, colder up there amongst times of the sky where they sail in colliding bands and gathering grasps, grasps like a cold and tired hand. Sun-rays speed through the fluid gaps between their bodies and they are pushed apart by a force of light. That is how weightless they seem: light moves them. In a collective effort of sapped strength they join together and fall down out of

73

the light and into tiered planes of shadow layering the early winter sky like strata as the geology of the sky, and the wind is the excited and rapid archaeologist.

Towards where I stand transfixed by the water's edge the lapwings beat as though they beat with a single pair of wings that governs them. They show obedience and the big pair of wings funnels them down in fumes of smoke and race toward me, compacting and hardening into a planetary meteorite burning bright and blinding white like unrolling coils of magnesium in a fire. At a focal point in the sky hundreds of feet away and up, suddenly a weightlessness takes hold of them and the white fire of themselves fizzles out and they drift along in a long pale gesture of sleep. It is as if they died on the wing. One by one they are revived by a stroke of genius. I thought they might have showered down like strobe rain, a slow-motion rainfall of lapwings swept along in a burst tombola that spins them around. No, they fly. With breathless professionalism they alight in pairs, threes, fours, and more where other lapwings have settled in for the night beside the lagoon.

Lapwings exist and cease in rhythms that I will never get used to but will always hold an endless fascination for. They confound me in their grace and in their unpredictable applications of strength. Their movement is the life of wisdom itself. Is it too much to shed a tear for one, if not all, these creatures? Ask me to kneel before them and I would, gladly.

≈

Lapwings squeal as though in pain and at play, as though playing with the feelings of pain as gulls and crows attack them for their eggs. Gulls, in scavenging packs, feral curs of the air, glide in from their islands, breach the mainland, and harass the lapwings in a riotous strategy of nuisance and threat. Lapwings guard their eggs by means of exaggerated gymnastics. One scraggy winged gull breaks away from its gang and corkscrews towards a lapwing that rises, beats, and lollops up to meet it wing on wind. What do they look like to each other in that crash collision of wing? Contending with much air and drag, the gull and lapwing swiftly tack and sway, and the gull is left with the open target of the egg. Then, from behind the gull, the lapwing squeals and rolls over repeatedly in untidy somersaults. Retorting with an asthmatic yelp the gull cannot help but turn away from the egg and face its adversary. Other lapwings rise up from the ground like a resurrection of acrobatic ghosts and by the shared grace of their plump precision of intent and action, the gull retreats and re-groups with its mob that's busily bothering other birds. The lapwings triumphed and I am pleased for them, but the drama will continue and will always continue.

Scooping sunlit air onto the wings and as they tilt in various directions no compass of mine could track, they drift down in an aftermath state of panic then, in a soothing bustle of wings, settle upon the battled ground.

I cannot tire from watching the lapwing's display of courtship, courage, and fear. Full of sheer ease that I feel – in full attention of them, as a strain in my own fibres and nerves and thoughts, I yearn to acquire at least a flicker of their statures and styles of being-in-the-world. Looking in on their world whilst the sea raps upon the sea-wall behind me, there is a joy I feel that begins to dawn up through me equivalent to a sphere of light no bigger, no smaller than my heart. The longer I watch and pay full attention to this place and the creatures of this place, the brighter and warmer the sphere of light becomes. The inward, glowing light is a collateral product of incantatory Being.

≈

The curlew's warble burns the air like a splash of freezing water onto the air's tender and bruised flesh. Echoing further on past where I can see to, the trilling song remains in the present like the aftermath of absolute loss. It speaks of loneliness and of irretrievable happiness.

The curlew cradles herself in bunches of seaweed that tassel the base of the sea-wall revealed at lowest tide. At lowest tide she strides out and lunges across the sleek and wet marble of the grey and brown mud-flats. Patting her feet on the mud to quake awake a burrowed worm that she will eat in the sunlight, she calls out to let the world know her sadness is true. Her song is the sound of the yearning of time, time that searches everywhere like a cold mist searching for the eternity that will dissipate it into a bright release.

≈

There is that bird of the salt-marshes I will never see but which I nonetheless wait for.

On the brink of leaping up, the visible world of the marshes trembles with a heightened pinch of electric being, at the pressing anticipation (I included) of the invisible birds constant, withheld arrival.

Beyond names, beyond image and body and colour and yet palpable in its intimate remoteness, I am geared towards that absence of wings which I believe, in my most innocent, naïve and simple moment, will flash down amongst here like lightning.

≈

Listening to lapwings in the dark, streams of geese overhead swerve, veer, and swing out toward a distant island at the river's mouth where the sea flows to where I should be in commune with a different night: another life in a different dark where stars are a local passion of feeling and wind-racing is a compulsory sport, and the clock- time will be told by the patterns of wings in the air. In dream, in imagination, I go there but those meagre fantasies bred upon a non-committal relationship to reality, buckle under the insistent clamour of the real.

That place and state is only one right thought away, that place wherein all things belong to one another. But where, and when, and how, to arrive at that one right thought? Is it the thought of darkness in which all thought is done and one's life is propelled forth into the One Life? Even the geese haven't got there yet, and the lapwings rise and fall, rise and fall. I was surprised to find that

Heraclitus said 'Wisdom is one thing: it is to know the thought by which all things are steered through all things.'

≈

The earth, through these mapped acres of the salt marsh, has gripped me more than I will ever know. Is it too much to worship a place, to take for a place one's own open-air cathedral, to transport them beyond the map into a region no coordinates can contain? Trusting in what I have undergone and what I will undergo here I have no scruples in calling myself, as Wordsworth did, 'a worshipper of nature.'

Earth is replete with signs I will never be able to read. So be it. I too, want to be a sign that cannot be read, written by the earth itself.

≈

Oystercatchers, in sixes, pipe and bleat, and swifts, swallows, sandmartins, house-martins, ride a carrousel of midges above Keyhaven Lagoon. The tall green grasses beneath them sway and crawl on the air. I grow dizzy watching them fly like a spun crown. It is quite impossible to keep my eye on one amongst the hundreds. They out skip my eyes and leave me muddled, bemused at my own failure to take them in. Instead of trying to focus on one, I step back to take in the whole spectacle. That, too, is awesome but the litheness of one is lacking. Neither in close nor out far, I find a perfect middle ground measured out for me by them. A sense much deeper and less decrepit than sight becomes engaged, and I feel and see all of them *and* a single one, in that deep distance where I stand, or, more accurately, I am *emplaced*. What is that sense that is used by the creatures to ensure that I can see and feel them in no better way imaginable?

≈

The heron, patiently dedicated to its spot by the sluice edge caught in the rush of the undertow of an outgoing tide, draws me in. Along with my vision and my own time, the sparse and wind-harried gorse, the crooked oak and papery bouquet of hollow reeds, the sprite teal and fluttering godwit, are pulled into the space of the heron's exactness. We are the shoal in its expanding net of stillness that is not drawn all the way up to the toggle of her mind but stops short at an optimum of liaise. She is doing hardly anything and yet she seems to be doing everything she can as she waits tall like a daggered column of blue and grey feathers balanced on an extremely sensitive spring. Does she see her image in the dark water? I imagine she sees straight through it into the inner artery of the water, because the water flows along the back of her eyes. Her eyes are of the water. The ignorant minnows are already borne along her vision and hooked onto the barbs of her nerve-endings. She is a rod, tense for the catch. The sword-end tip of her bill dangles above the streams that, at any moment, could fall like a spike. Relaxed and yet every muscle and nerve tense for the lancing stab, the heron is in complete physical balance with where and what she is.

Drawn in by her subtle magnetism, I watch, waste my time to a point of timelessness, wait in anticipation for the unfulfilled promise of wonder. Like a budding contemplative, I am undergone by the world stretched taut to a pitch pregnant with anticipated song. What will break forth? When will the seams of the world burst apart for a unique beam of light to scintillate the sky? She keeps me guessing; that is her manoeuvre. She is a blue and grey flame I meditate upon to move myself into a shared space of stillness where she too fully abides. A hero of contemplative practice the heron binds the world of brown weak reed and wave and I about her and, in the same stroke, lets us go. She breathes the world toward her and away with a fluidity that is entirely natural.

My stamina of attention falters after a while of heron-gazing or, perhaps she is far too implacable and stand-offish. At that point when I become aware of myself as a separate specimen of existence, her head jolts down and the lance of her bill rises dripping with a silver and sunlit minnow wriggling and wriggling. It was as though the elasticity between us snapped and the trap of her bill plummeted into the sluice, into the heart of the world that is not wooded but woken, shocked into animation. The tension that bristled upon my skin from watching her dissipates, my neck muscles relax from the isotonic strain. I blink many times to massage the pressure out of my eyes that had been building up, accumulating, in the stare. Released from the grip of her stillness, I stand up, knees creaking, and walk away fatigued and exhilarated.

In his book *The Inward Morning*, Henry Bugbee talks of the 'innermost spring of responsiveness.' Locating it, that spring of responsiveness most sensitive to the yank of the real requires that practice of sustained, obedient attention that I undergo in sharing in the heron's watch, herself a watchtower and the watcher.

I look back over my shoulder to see if she is still there by the sluice gate and she is until, by some inner necessity, she lifts and rises, bounces on layered trampolines of air then floats, languidly flopping her wings now and again over Keyhaven Lagoon toward the woods. Her gruff squawk resounds through me like an echo searching for its source and, for some lunatic reason, by squawking back the echo within is freed back toward her as she floats down to a clearing in the woods in the style of a moon-landing. For a moment I possessed the language of wings, of heron, even.

≈

The curlew's song is the sound of the wind playing the carbon harp of her bill as she tries to pencil her name into the skull-grey sky with thick ink of black and brown mud. Haunting to her, a wail like a child lost on the marsh or caught in a quick sand in this lonely land of grey, the lead mist engulfs the marshes. Through the mists a far off fog-horn blasts like a god of ghosts summoning back his revenant patrol. The curlew's song is the song I wish to hear at the end of the world.

≈

I could spend my days here attuning the rhythms of my body and thoughts to the rhythms of the blown reed and the heavy bird below the sagging train of clouds. A romantic idea of course, but one I have seriously considered.

Waiting for the next cormorant to fill the space of my concentration becomes, in that moment, the most important event in my life. And then, like a surplus of blessing, a gust off the sea whooshes through the reeds and the soul-stirring sounds are almost unbearable in their beauty but, in a few methodical breaths, I ease into the raucous of the world and find, at the heart of it, a limitless and passionate order.

≈

I have far to go but the heron by the mud-flat stream is there.

≈

I plunge my hand into the floury piles of shells that line the small beach at the head of Keyhaven Lagoon. Out from the lucky dip I bring a shell swirled with multiple shades of magenta and sparkling purples and green, the core-tip of which is a diamond glinting point. Sea-worn jewels; an endless treasure. The shells look and feel expensive. Handling one with precise care from the tumbled casket of shells and sand, I slip it into my pocket like a grateful thief. The design of them astounds me; the carat of them is beyond fathoming. They are light shapes of ceramic air shaped by spray and wind and time in the wild whirl of pottery and sculpture. In a high southwest wind the petal-light shells are tossed across the beach. I could spend days here amongst the shells and become an expert of their finery, details, and ages. Sometimes I am so lost in my world that I become convinced that a community could trade in these shells instead of money.

≈

I remember on one of those clear and bright days of noon-sun as I walked toward Keyhaven, surrounded by flocks of lapwings and plovers flashing back and forth in rapid zig-zags over the sea, I felt a presence of wind. But there was no wind because every reed and feather was still. A power wide and strong, a volume of a nameless element, flowed in from the glowing horizon of the open sea that troughed and curled beyond Hurst Spit and the Needles.

In a hallucinatory vibrancy, the power affected not only me but a V of geese. It blew them apart, breaking the bonds between them. Lagoon waves rose and rolled spluttering along the chunks of the cement sea-wall, turnstones crouched for their tiny lives in their feed dens, huddled between loads of seaweed and driftwood, the cross-shaped mud-flat danger-sign rattled and groaned. Daylight was rushed to brighten and brighten by these arias and compelling shocks of non-air that delivered the sound of a distant rumbling wind. Blasted characters, the birds, with hawk-quick looks held fast in the racked corridors of a shaken world, an airy mansion almost torn to shades and ashen pieces. Egrets, herons, deftly fought for their guardianships of stillness and silence as I emerged on my inter-rupted walk from behind candle-crowned gorse, lit and hit once as firmly as a punch right here, beside the heart, by a calm but sure-winged hand. More of an interlocked sequence of daydreams than a rollicking of real events, that windless day of power and presence was the residual breath of a vestigial god I was close to summoning back into the hearth of the world by simply being there, by simply, as Robinson Jeffers puts it, 'falling in love outward.'

≈

At Keyhaven Harbour fish sip at hulls, masts tilt and clack like a children's night-time mobile, a sleepiness pervades every stone and wave. A salt suffused breeze whisks by with a fatigued cormorant in it. A coiled rope suns itself on the jetty after this morning's forecast downpour. Children, as I once was here with good friends and family, dangle crab-lines down from crackle-paint railings, their blue buckets are filled with promises of water: two buckets of sky the crabs will fly in. Mid-air, a green-crab falls twirling with a soggy bacon-rind pinched between its pincers. The children shout at the same time the crab plops into the water.

A bright blue net like a mapped sky but fainter is being mended on the jetty by two tattooed men dipping, pulling bunched instruments of twine through and over stippled stitching; a constant and silent music heralding the healing of the day. One of the men stops, flicks his cigarette butt – a pleasure relic – into the glowing air, its ember-tip spins past an old man's face like a thrown clock-hand, a face whose eyes are closed in deep and painful contentment.

The dark peace of things as they are is the wisdom the old man sees as the cigarette, a time-piece burning out, sizzles in a puddle on the jetty flank. A swan drifts across his mind like an angel at home on earth. Harbour fish bob up through reflected clouds, masts clack, distant reeds seethe and sigh, seethe and sigh. The universe breathes. Bounds break away and dissolve in the infinite.

≈

I have been watching the egret for a while and I cannot get over how radiant she is even on a day overthrown by an anaemia of light. No moon this autumn morning, but the egret perching at the fringe of the lagoon is as white and as still as an animal of the moon. After lifting her left foot above the dull water, then bathing it back dripping into the slow flow, her eyes close. No ripples fan out from where her foot slipped back in towards the water's soft edge, curved like the side of a violin. Oystercatchers, sensing that a disturbing quake of stillness will soon pervade nearby territories, leave and pipe all the way to where they go.

She makes me think what she feels so calmingly in her furious ease in the stretched-star fled water whether a creature as quiet as her qualifies as ceasing to exist. She might be a god. She might burst apart in an explosion of satin sheeted light any second now. How dark and deep is the dark and deep within and around her? The milligram weight of her headdress flapping in the breeze doesn't distract her from her work. If she is not hunting or sleeping what, on earth, is she doing?

≈

Here as I wander amongst the flat land of broad horizons and horizontal cleaves of light and vertical shots of wings for the umpteenth time, watching gulls wheel around the sun in vacant hypnotism, and see a flash of the dunlin's underwing over the weed stuffed stone, listening to the solent sea slap against the sea-wall and feel the immensity of the sky volley away into unimaginable distances, I am overcome by what John Muir called 'the invincible gladness.' Everything around me from the merest glint of shell to the grandest motion of the wind and sea and flight of the birds in the eddying parlours absorbs me into an element that stands and partakes of all elements, a continuation and enveloping and of fire, water, air, and earth. I can hear the cheep of the greenshank as it lift all legs from the sluice edge through the hall of space no less than the booming wave that passes in whispers. Injected by a kind of starlight in a boundless moment of gladness, I partake of the earth through the portal of this seemingly unremarkable place and feel the course of evolution bustle through my blood and brain.

≈

I saw an osprey only once here, using these marshes as a pit-stop on its way south. I knelt when I saw, but by the time I knelt she flew away high into the distance. I ran to catch up with her, but she was gone. I write of her now:

In my mind's eye she is a kaleidoscope of Being. Let me admire you, the way you see daylight as I would read an answer, the way your broad wing arrests and worries the air to obey your weight is the way I will touch my first child's head of hair. I see how it is you speak, Osprey. Your body is a mill of delicate, furious beauty. Your black ball bearing of an eye is a pulse spoked by a spiked iris of a million green-gold hues that quivers or rests as if in command of a lull or leap in today's weather. This moment is your climate. Foresights of blustering open a fishes throat, keeps you tense and ready. Your far-off nest of flensed brawn needs refilling. Each fibre's inner fire is blazing, but your feathers are slack and cool. The swell of the sea beneath where you scan equates with the swell of my heart when you lift, Osprey, then spin down, a visible volt, to vanish in a flash-dive through sun enamelled mist. You almost take me with you until I'm caught in a trance of imagining what it is you leave behind in flight – a vapour trail of colours we are when we turn in sleep, turn through towards the clues of first light, gripping onto the first thing we see in a daze of worship. I hope that I will return, and I will be there more in time to see you.

꒪

From cold cruel waters, the cobalt coil of the kingfisher springs up with her catch, throttling low over pools. The pools are too slow to reflect her blue wings and belly of amber gold. She darts down streets crowded with birds silly-drunk with jealousy, through cities of sky-scraping reeds blown back quaking by the silent, Chinook-thrumming of her wings.

She flies as though pursued, in fear of being mugged. Whipping, dabbing, and dodging, shocking the heron from his deep midday meditation. She alights, shakes out the icicle light that the bouncing moon of the egret borrows for his brightness, and the curlew is inspired to shoot mud stars into the night's canvas from the bow of his bill, and the sea approaches in slow and excited tides to witness her sleeping.

Each wave takes turns to hold, nurse, and freshen her from afar. Her colours need dream-time to repair. And then, suddenly, she will wake, break through the gawking awestruck world, catching everything off guard, except for the morning sun that has waited all night to throw a sparkling new dress upon her, to coil down into cold cruel waters, to seduce and kiss a catch disguised as a brooch in the summer sky of her hair.

꒪

I stand out on the concrete jetty that juts out from the little beach of shells into the middle of the Solent. Surrounded by sea and light and salt-air and the motions of the heavens above and the feeling of the open sea dancing out beyond the spit. It is hard not to be elated by mere existence. 'Being, not doing, is my first joy,' as Roethke wrote.

Everything seems to be moving steadily towards some great culmination of existence, wherein all things shall shoot through all things in an ultimate intensity of oneness and difference.

The curlew calls, the avocet appears in another avocet's wake as though pieced together by a hand of moonlight and shadow, and the cormorant dries its plate-stiff wings on the sea-wall, and I stand there, at the edge of things on the long jetty's steep edge, letting the dynamic energy of life pour through me. I am not there at all but I am there, *here*, itself. To others walking along the sea-wall with their dogs and binoculars I must cut an odd figure out there with my arms out in a stance of surrender, sacrifice.

Once, in these exhilarations, I saw my grandfather, my mother's father, down below in a small skiff with oars on the water. He loved birds too, and the land, and sea. Then a sideways rainfall of light erased him, but I felt strongly the presence of an ancestor who acted as a guide to the deeper places but which, up until then, I had not been aware. The right people can make me feel as though I belong.

The motion of the waves continued and will continue until the earth comes to an end and the egrets shall lift the bright trophies of themselves into the hands of the sky, and the reeds shall blow a thousand hurried stories until all is obliterated by the changes that define the universe. Until that catastrophe I shall keep my head down amongst the water and mud and carry on trying to get close enough to the world and to feel the graceful caress of feathers upon my closed eyes.

V

FORAGINGS

Be still, my heart, these great trees are prayers.
> —Rabindranath Tagore[1]

In this wilderness I have learned how to sleep again. I am not alien. The trees I know, the night I know, the rain I know. I close my eyes and instantly sink into the whole rainy world of which I am a part, and the world goes on with me in it, for I am not alien to it.
> —Thomas Merton[2]

1ST OCT 13

Every morning I humbly and quietly re-introduce myself to the earth. Walking the sloping lane towards the sun kindling at the ragged heart of the wood, beneath an onward rolling blue sky, I breathe deeply enough to feel at peace with what I am and where I am in this very moment.

2ND OCT 13

The contribution I make to Being is perfectly minimal, and what I gain is also perfectly minimal. I am simply here. Nothing added, nothing taken away. Or so I would like to think. Bearing no gifts other than this vaguely definable presence that I am, the earth, through grass-blade, falling autumn leaf, cloud and sky and flicking air, remembers me. Or so I would like to think.

4ᵀᴴ OCT 13

This local beam of earth transfigured into an autumn wood is a numinous realisation of itself through me, and every other thing in that wood.

The holy, the ineffable, the nameless hush of light that is the supporting spine of all things earthly, grubby and rough-edged – not God, no appellations – is registered, first of all, on the bristling skin, upon the rounded globe of a single goose bump swelling in the coaxing breeze, upon the tongue-tip, the lip and watery eye, and voluptuous lung. Continuity between *that*, which cannot be named and *this* which lends itself to be named, is safeguarded by this body that I am.

6ᵀᴴ OCT 13

I love the trees, the shades, and depths of light the trees create and conjure, the careless litter of crab-apples, the steaming warmth of bogged-down bracken piles in the cool mists of, what seems like, a premature morning. I love the shades of water, the whole music of hapless gushing and lapping, the touch of coarse sand beneath the arched foot that curves like an ear pressed down upon secret, enormous melodies. I love it all.

I am happiest when I love the earth and not afraid to use such an overblown verb. A butterfly upon a dying flower is as awesome as the mountain that no butterfly may ever alight upon.

Amidst all this passion, the golden maxim surfaces: love of life depends upon the premise of accepting things as they are. One cannot love life if one cannot accept things as they are. Passion must be worked out, without it shrinking into calculation.

9ᵀᴴ OCT 13

Autumn. There's a lilting breeze to that word, a sinking and drifting cadence. Deer walk as quietly as leaves fall, their feet tapping away into the distance. Soft brilliance of the sun upon strong green leaves, the last bundle of them, as everywhere and elsewhere the red and orange showers, the blushed carmines and yellow crimsons.

From the darkness, with its golden glow of a spread hand, my heart – or an organ near to my heart – is roused into equanimity. Trying to hold onto this buoyancy of calm only nudges it further away. Let it come, let it go, my will obedient to that ebb and flow.

Walked on passed elm and holly and squat oaks tangled amidst oaks, branches washed by autumn rain, the dead leaves of my being go to the ground to be restored whilst I am more exposed to myself, to something other. I see the deer more clearly because of my breakdown into bareness; straight past the congestion of my own self into deer and the world sharing itself between us.

10ᵀᴴ OCT 13

As Wallace Stevens puts it: 'to exist in the world and yet outside any conceptions of it.' Evasion, then, on my part, of concepts is supported by the conspiracy of things – the conspiracy of things being the ways in which they conceal their essences from prying eyes that desire to extract the living ore from things and set them up in cold dead galleries of the intellect. The conspiracy of things as they are is the good crime against man's arrogance.

Is it not imperative in keeping with the above strategy to be eccentric to explanations, yet central, integral to participation?

To let these woods become my home more intimately than my own blood is my aim. Who is there to instruct and guide me?

11ᵀᴴ OCT 13

Sky surrounding me, my feet embracing the mud, my lungs replete with cold autumn air, the sweetness of it making my mind laugh – how can I not be content? Pain, yes, comes my way in no short measure but dissolves into this blessed solution of body-world rapport.

There is liberation to be found in knowing that *here* is the only place I can ever be. Elsewhere is imprisonment.

Fresh russet sunrise, ragged cloud-rims gilt mercury and boldly embossed with watery lines. Two tacking and jolting herons flew high above and over the road at home in the wayward, boisterous infinity that tussles everywhere. And a rainbow in the slight film of passing rain! Sense of grounded and elated calm; the whole day remaining to muse upon this hour.

One more heron – dark spectre in darker dusk – floated above the wood. Veering away she spied me then glided toward the exploded oak that was jostling in the wind.

12TH OCT 13

Morning breezes, between-branch cast, leaf-wide and long as the alleyway that stretched between trunks and replenished by the winds blustering down from dispersed canopies above. It caressed my bare arms as I held them out in front and traipsed down the warm lane through four, no, five horses tearing stubbed grass.

Exhilarating to see the sky, monumental blue, at the same time that acorns and raindrops and crab-apples thudded in off-time with each step. Ethereal sounds. Walking on solid air. Clear clean notes of a wren in a hideaway.

A mere hour's walk, the same round I repeat so often and find in a short distance of time, not dullness, but a length and breadth of experience I have rarely encountered in other domains of the holy, the visceral hush, the barking silence. Such expansion in such autumnal minutiae.

What is this delight or joy I feel in mere existence, and the sadness or frustrated confusion that comes when I am not, by some interruption, permitted to be simply as I am, as I be? In what ways am I broken? Towards what vision shall I re-make myself, and in re-making myself what will happen to the world I have come to know? A discrete effervescence trembles within each thing eager to be sipped by lips that are eager to purse the shape of silence.

13TH OCT 13

Without this one leaf, I am not.

At what point shall the restoration of myself, and thus the renewal of the sacred, undergo itself? It begins closer than the eye, than one's breath. Move a tittle of thought and I miss it by aeons.

There seems to be no end to how closely I can come into contact with things. This point of re-birth is none other than the space in which all things from star to grass-blade tip are one and intensely different. I feel that I am nearing, through simply paying attention beyond myself into the collapsing labyrinth of this autumn wood, the source, the boundless circle of light.

14TH Oct 13

The thinning of autumn. The incipient fullness of spirit.

A kingfisher, chip of sapphire jewel, sky-droplet, rattled a foot or so above the ground, zipping like a dragonfly bloated on its own beauty toward the darkness of the wood and the darkness of the sluggish, zinc-tinted stream. Flying from lightness to darkness, itself a torch of itself, at what slim stage, how far from the darkness of the wood does the dear bird's pupils begin to dilate?

Like a thief, stealing the treasure of its self along, it is quiet with accomplished escape, not wanting to be seen by a being like I who cannot be a torch unto itself. But how easy it is to see the kingfisher! It cannot hide, its beauty is its flaw, an attraction that does not wish to attract while it hunts.

What does seeing, looking, bending an eye towards that shockingly beautiful bird do to me? What effect does it have on me, a kingfisher-witness, and on the little world of the one glugging stream, and autumn branch bereft of dangling leaves, those sun spades shovelling in the goodness?

The mystery of things as they are is gaining in clarity but really has nothing to do with sight as I have been reared up to think of it. I see it, the mystery more mysteriously urgent because of its clarity, and I feel it pervading the supple netted network of nerve and bone hitched to the creaking joint of things lubricated by light, the blood of God.

I am seized by a hunger to know all things, and for that hunger to be satisfied by not knowing. No, here in this round hope of woodland is a knowledge so simple that it could easily be mistaken for a frivolous encumbrance of the real matter of the world, a shimmering strap of tinsel around the broad neck of buff 'truth.' I do not know what it is, but I know how it is in its generosity. It is a non-light

light, a non-presence presence, but not an absence. To attempt to submit myself to it – the wonderfully inexplicable – is an attempt I must repeat as often as I grind the bone of my jaw.

I love that I have found this other side to life, but I have done nothing outrageous to receive such a perspective. I have certainly not been 'chosen' in any sense of that term. How can such a low-key extravagance of spirit visit me in this small, inconsequential world of one garden, some trees, and a lane?

At times a coldness blows through me, horse-bone grey and damp, a dying thing, a blind badger lost from its burrow, like the afterlife of a forgotten dream insisting to be remembered, it haunts me but does not abide, does not persuade to be settled. Dejected, it goes its own way torn at the sides. That is 'I,' the purblind martyr, wailing, mouthing into the wheel of disarray. Being hums.

15ᵀᴴ Oct 13

Cawing crows spiralled out of the lane-side oak in a single black ribbon or like pan-sized black leaves caught in an updraft, unlocked and loosened from their perch-snags by the rattling keys of the wind.

What will bud in their place, a dark trace or a sign? What is the scent of an autumn crow? Are its wings as fragrant as the dying sweetness of this heady air? What is the perfume of flight, this lightness I feel in my limbs when I watch them elevate in the element that knows them well? Their spiralling disbands into an across-field scattering and the lane is sombre with the memory of their song.

All around me as I walk, my feet dripping, and look and listen and touch and taste, through this autumn vector of wood, the motion of everything returning to itself is that of a seemingly inevitable wheel turning and beating like an archetypal heart that births forth the inseparable bloom of space and time.

16ᵀᴴ Oct 13

Vivid fresh clean day. Consciousness a ripening blue fruit of the sky.

Having located the door to autumn and walked straight (with a few detours) through, the imperative to let myself be cast, to surrender, moulded into a pliant receptacle of the holy by autumn's graft, has become as pressing and as certain as the impending horizon of winter. I stand and wait and obey in the weakening folds of light.

17TH OCT 13

Rain. Light leaves falling amongst heavy rain, slow motion amidst hurry and velocity. No wind but every clinging leaf struck and swaying in the wind-wide rain.

I feared that nothing would come of my walk today due to the rain and absence of actual light. Entering the broad bridleway over-arched with beech and ash and birch and oak then re-entering the clumped wood proper toward home I was overcome – on no conscious part of my own – by the exhilarating emergency of need, desire, eros, to dive ever more profoundly into the sensations of a moment. Tears almost swelled to my eyes as I breathed, breathed in the autumn air and felt the continual dragonfly clipping of rain upon my upturned face. I stopped. I lifted my sodden arms out either side of body and turned my hand this way and that. The joy! The bliss of plunging ever more deeply into that bliss! The contact!

What faculty is it that registers and responds to that bliss? Surprising how much one can undergo on a supposedly uneventful walk in woods seen over and over again.

By noon, rain ceased and quickly blue sky resumed the water-logged hush. Late afternoon up Manor Farm lane, strong wind from nowhere turbulent in the oak leaning over the road. Small sun descending over wet fields. Pleasure to stand and lean upon a crooked gate and look out over radiant fields.

Compulsion, then, to follow every nerve-racking sense to its extremest point, its deepest most furthest end where I will be hurled, vertiginously, into the foray of the incomprehensible: the bluest sky, the greenest field, the calmest heart, the fullness of world and non-I surging in waves, in darkness, rallying towards the Source. No arrival but an exasperating constant delivery towards God or the nameless body of mystery that animates every thing into a perfect safekeeping of light.

18ᵀʰ Oct 13

I sit alone in the darkness upon a log. Three tea-lights quiver upon three upturned flowerpots. Brown spiders work on their webs in the corner above a bird's nest. The shriek of an owl echoes – the ghost of its voice gone into time's spectre-breached canyons.

My own breathing is strange to me; the air is not mine.

Stars bud bare branches. I close my eyes slowly and earnestly in the shelter and sit hunched over with my forearms resting lightly upon the insides of my knees. It is not cold. It is not warm. I blow out the little flames, cancelling the shadows. All is darkness. The wood encloses me in its cocoon, its autumn womb. I am erased.

How old am I here in this darkness and quiet? Who is it that presses these feet upon the moist leaves? What is this rocking element wherein I become estranged from myself and yet in the same movement (though I am still, so still) I am united with something that knows me more that I know myself? Why is there comfort in this solitude?

Returning to the beginning that will never end, always beginning, the first sign of life, is a real enchantment I have woken up to in this withdrawn space with my eyes closed, enfolded in darkness, the music of rustling night-leaves, all closed in and all opened out.

I look forward to the evenings when I can sit alone in the shelter that teaches me nothing.

20ᵀʰ Oct 13

Today I looked deeply into the incomprehensible.

For the first time the darkness was iridescent with a light that was no light – a vivid husk – that I have known and yet it was not alien or remote. It was near like the darkness itself, at first a vague, scattered shimmering like a haunting squall of indefinite stars searching for one another to compact itself into fixity, constellation.

The longer I looked the more I did not understand.

The darkness rejoiced with light that was beam-direct and impartially enveloping, not harsh but forgiving, knowing, wise. Because of this virtue of darkness I now no longer yearn for light outright. I yearn for the dark in which the light abides, becomes. Am I on the right track? Is my spirit colour blind?

The leaves fall, whispering to one another the stories that will be told about them years hence from now. And to think that two leaves from distant trees collide in the wind and twirl down in a spread helix of fitful meeting, eroding into the very soil that fed them. Think of it.

The undulating, intersecting cycles continue even for 'I' as I loop down into a vital darkness, the 'I' dissolved, eaten away into disintegration, for the forest of light to sprout, flourish and groan amidst the autumn wood that acts as a blue-print for the numinous architecture to heed. Think of it.

21ST OCT 13

Go plant the seed of the nothing that I am. Dig out the soil with the shovel of hands in prayer. Step aside. Let the light stream in through the wasting canopy of the mind. Surrender to the wind and rain that whips one bare. In bareness begins the blossoming, the summoning of God to itself through me – autumn's medium.

22ND OCT 13

The wind surging through the trees makes me think and feel the sweep of waves across seething shingle that bright day when we walked together, Mother and I, along the beach. I wanted to hold her hand, to hold her close to me. Did she want to hold mine? I remember gulls silently wheeling around and through the southwest wind as we drifted off toward one another in the vast circumference of blue, and gold, and white nativity.

23RD OCT 13

When will I know when I am not apart from these woods?

We do not see deeply into things when we travel broadly over them, skim-read, as it were, certain places. There are places we must stay with for the good of our soul. These places will accept you when they know that you know them. I do not mean 'know,' in the sense of taxonomy and objective reduction of things into categories. That type of knowing is still very much locked in the knower's version of things. Staying with a certain place for as long as the place asks you yields a sense of knowing not based on testable facts but a knowing that share's in the life of love, of mutual release and growth. Let places, let these woods that could easily be measured in terms of number and quantity but immeasurable in terms of spiritual depth, breathe its life into you. Let its moods overshadow yours. Stay put. Be moved into the place where all things thrive. When it knows you mean business, these places will unveil their inner light to you. I am sure of it.

24ᵀᴴ Oct 13

Sidling from dense oak-crowds and burly beeches into skeletal, silver-birch groves is a subdued, eerie experience, spooky and beguiling. In them, birdsong seems far away even though the birds are so close I can see their beaks gleam with the rime of song. The world disbands, something less substantial contracts in its place, a something reliant on sound to find its way through from wherever it lingered or strayed.

Tall, tatty, thin and gaunt, the highest leaves rustle but are too high to see trembling. Touch and sight turns obsolete, the ear becomes paramount.

The sparse grove harbours in its weakness a presence that is a trace, an incomplete sketch of itself that flees but ends up as a nowhere, a grey fatigue. The trees are question marks curling over under their own weight. The only answers are the winds that are scraps of yesterday's air trying to catch up with today's.

Is it the wisp-cloud covered moonlight colour of the peeling bark, slashed with black rot that envelops each silver birch with a puckered skin of mystery? It is a cemetery alive with the unborn.

Whisperings, stuttered secrets, frail poltergeists, and anaemic spirits slouch amongst the branches. Anorexia of time: enlargement of a non-time, not eternity, but still persisting in time, in materiality. The birches inhabit a space between eternity and time, lingering where they cross, a breath floating in purgatory speaking words that have never existed.

Autumn, hearse of haze, makes of the grove a mistiness, an atmosphere of ill, like the sense of self in a dream in which one acts and withdraws simultaneously. Being all body, I ease through the silver birches; a realm of lapse in the clamouring scheme of things.

A cool element disturbed by its owness ferries me through back into the hardened world of oak. Touch and sight returns as natural as reflex at the knock of the real. I thank the ear for being the guide between worlds within worlds.

25TH OCT 13

Seeing the tender ferns that have yet to rust into crisp bones of bracken, and hearing the brisk power of the stag as it thuds away into the distance, its antlers clicking against the antlered branches, transports me back to an autumn of my school days in these very same woods. I cannot recall what the purpose of the trip was but I remember feeling joy in the woods.

In pairs we built shelters. Ours mainly consisted of moss brickwork, a roof, and dehorned branches stuffed with insulation of moss, moss, and more moss. The musty fragrance of it stitched itself into my ivory-skin hands. After constructing a shelter we were let loose, or so it seemed to me, into a region of the forest still visible to the teacher's eye. A tea-brown stream rushed over golden-brown pebbles. Across from the stream over a green clearing a fallen oak, gnarled root-base protruding, caught my eye and I went running. Knee-deep in what seems now like luminous pool-green fern that had splashed up around the trunk, I tip-toed along the round rough plank of bark and up to the very top, its branches on the earth like hands pausing mid-dig, and stood there quite amazed at the top of the oak that reached no higher than my child-self from the soil.

A wicked stench injected body rot into air drained of its freshness, and I peered over into the sea of ferns to spot the foul cause. A dead stag, newly dead, drowned in the green. Ferns crushed beneath its bulk, the twisted shape of him impressed there. Hopping down I first inspected the crooked swords of his antlers. His open black eyes were beyond vacancy. A red-butter gash of a wound wended its way from back leg along centre belly to foreleg. Ants and maggots erratically ploughed the blood furrow.

In a deliberate privation of hesitancy, I grabbed the longest antler-prong and hauled the sack of him through the fern that obediently parted either side of my determined path. I felt strong, brave and courageous. Slinging his floppy head down into the clearing all the other children flocked to see the hunter and his hunted. Some gasped in disgust, some fled to snitch on my misdemeanour. They should've knelt before the Child-Lord of Stags, or so I daydreamed as I swayed there buzzing with excitement and triumph that was soon deflated into shame and embarrassment when the teacher came huffing along pointing her brazen and enormous finger.

26ᵀᴴ Oct 13

Wherever I walked this morning I broke spider webs, silver strings glinting and floating in the windless air, so light they seemed moved by light and moved, too, to an inaudible exertion of music.

Did not Coleridge, in a moment of lucidity, proclaim 'A light in sound, a sound-like power in light?' Are not lightness and grounded step the measureless qualities of the soul? Is not walking, looking, all modes of participation, an integral dance with, what Coleridge also said, 'The One Life within us and abroad?'

I have found in these woods that contemplation is an act of re-aligning the basic rhythms of one's life with the Life of the universe, leading on into the wild flow of the one Life that is the wholesome shape of God.

27ᵀᴴ Oct 13

Hearing about the arrival and settlement of goshawks in neighbouring woods I went in search of them. After a fruitless, blundering search through woods that I was ill acquainted with, I went instead to the small exhibition of goshawks that was being displayed down the road from here.

Overhearing talk between two experts about the failure of a

mother in abandoning her chick (or possibly the mother was stolen by thieves for eggs) I returned back to my woods and put out a vision of feeling for her and imagined the scenario. On occasion, if attuned right, the imagination can enter into sympathetic union with live beings. The rain was coming in strong and I imagined the goshawk chick frail and drenched in its cold nest. She should've hatched yesterday before today's rains arrived riding on a drumming westerly. I focused on the image of the rain soaking the papery shells of the chick's eyelids that were as thin as tracing paper. I wanted to go look for the mother.

28ᵀᴴ Oct 13

Easy buzzard crying out in the chill space of the sky, drifting in liquid thermals upward and over the skittish trees.

Buzzard's-eye view of these woods, the barer the better for she to see the vulnerable. The brink of winter brings her consolations, the agreement between the tail-end of autumn and the mouth of the ice snake that is winter unfurling, uncurling on the horizon of seasons.

She cries again, this note plaintive, mournful. Her idiolect is one of the wood's dialects and vice versa. Her song trills my nerves, particularly the nerves in my neck, the arms, and legs. The idea of flight is the colour of gladness.

I wait with a blank mind for her next pitch. The expectancy is almost unbearable. The wood-world turns into a tuning fork. Tensions bristle.

Her song is an alarm of fulfilment for my patience, my devotion to a life beyond my capacity to know. Whether she sings or not I will be forever on the edge of my seat, of my being, so to speak. 'The meaning is in the waiting,' announced R. S. Thomas. Her song fills these woods of the sky even when no song is heard.

I figure that prayer is the vigilance of being arced towards an absence that valorises prayer into communion. Do these woods, of which I am a part, tingle like the hairs upon an arm brushed by the presence of God, by the melody of the buzzard's song? What is awareness when there is no being, no I, a nothing, to be aware? There is emptiness, the sky in every seed. There is enrichment, continuity.

The buzzard's song is a vision of the spiritual truth that in stillness, waiting, a sense of God is registered as certain as the stone is hard, grey, round. These woods have been good to me.

30ᵀᴴ Oct 13

Being here is enough. I am a being who does not pause to think, and if I pause it is only not to think. I am a being who does not desire to build up objects based on the fantasies of my desire. The richness of desire is its emptiness. Essentially, nowhere needs changing course.

I am a being for whom the god of earth is the flexing energy in the supple tendon of the stag as it bounds across a moonlight clearing panicked by an unfamiliar snap in the dark. My god is the *quietus* of adrenaline that surges and sparkles through every being. I am a being who is where he is, who does not hold onto where he is but who, stepping aside, gives where he is the room to be.

Grave and sunken coming winter sucks the autumn dregs from November-away into its hoarse and ancient mouth. Leaves fall, light streams in, shadows vie for shadows. My chest rises. I am quite, quite content. Everything is here. I happily do not know what anything is except I know where everything is because a light shines upon it. The woods are without bounds.

31ˢᵀ Oct 13

Clocks go back. Old Man Winter has his eye on the wood. The frail marauders of frost will soon resume the land.

I bury my head into the burrowed darkness of my shelter and think, intuit, upon what winter may bring. Repetition is the golden norm, the daily rituals of identification. Go barefoot in the cold. Try your hand upon the harps of ice.

What else is there for me to do but re-enact the day-to-day regime of every morning humbly and quietly re-introducing myself to the earth, walk the sloping lane towards the colder sun kindling at the ragged heart of the wood, beneath an onward rolling blue sky, and breathe deeply enough to feel at peace with what I am and where I am in this very moment.

VI

HOPE COTTAGE:
CONTEMPLATION'S HOME

Where are we really going? Always home.
—Novalis[1]

We must be still and still moving
Into another intensity
For a further union, a deeper communion . . .
—T. S. Eliot [2]

I found myself at the far end of the barn looking back at the house through the rain. Three lit windows were candles in the night. There was a warmth to that moment despite the cold heavy rain and wind arriving in from the wide-open heath. Behind me the darkness and loud rain made the paddock stretch away forever as though its bounds had been washed away – a sea at night far from land. I was peering into the darkness of a dreamless sleep. Whose mind was this? The woods breathed in the wind. A shower of rain flashed past into a vanishing burst. January's magic. The month of my deeper birth, the true self brought to light, the light of home.

I could have stood out in the night-rain for a long, long time leaning against the barn until the cold would've pinched my bones bloodless, closing my eyes now and again to compare the quality of the darkness without to the quality of the darkness within. Quiet kinship rolled from thing to thing. Yes, I could've stood there until time itself became the diagonal swiping rain, the high waving woods, the night-wind and glassy grain-field of the ground, giving up its nagging to meld into shapes of my new home. The spirit is patient. The need for home dispenses with waiting. It keeps up my desire, a desire not to have a home but to be home. Here itself is my shelter; *here* itself is the shelter of all things. Home is a temple to *here*.

Turning back, soaked away from the endlessness of the field and rain towards the house with its three lit windows like square motionless fires framed in silent songs of light, or lamps on a far shore dwelling to guide the sea-goer home, I realised that even when caught astray in a drag of emptiness, the painless wound that needs pain to heal, there is a hearth here, a sense of welcome. I think my deepest desire that rages on will be quelled here. I trust in what I see to put those flames out, to bring a clear space to my desire into which things may take root and grow, not to let desire stamp down a way for itself, crushing beneath its foot what in fact it most needs.

Gravel crunched beneath my feet. The motion-sensor light pinged on, catching me off guard in the house's vigil. I clasped the door-ring as though I were part of its anchorage for the first time. Inside was quiet and warm while outside rain rose and fell, rose and fell in waves of peace, a visible music of calm my heart of hearts knew as its truest pulse.

≈

Down in Studley Wood that borders the wild heath with tall elm, oak, beech, and ash, a brown brook, Latchmore Brook, is swerving around the long bends of slumped clay, solid grey clouds of it punctured by shafts of split oak like black tendrils. Around the bends the brook narrows and runs, undergoing itself with lifts of whispering wash, rain fed and slope coaxed. By many standards it is not an immediately beautiful river, a blue river running through a green valley of paradise, but this brown brook, two meters wide, half a metre deep, is my paradise. It is my place of innocence that cradles and lulls me in my desire to lay down with things, to let things hold and embrace, to quiet that restless determination to see things shake themselves asleep in the human shadow of control and power. Here, by this brown brook that flushes on, limp and weak, its current no more than what a child could muster with a bucket, I cast no shadow. Things awaken me to light, the smallest things force me to my knees and I am grateful, humble.

A buzzard mewed above the winter wood, a female, I think, rotating in wide circles, at first clockwise and then anti-clockwise. Hypnotic to watch, to fall under its spell. The brook ran on. I followed as many things as I could in their calling, their flushed being. There's a separateness to things in winter, a mood of sparseness that holds things apart not in terms of arrest and prevention but in aid and support, granting to each thing the room to roam, recover through their own uniquenesses on the brink of being wrested away into uniformity. Everything is on the brink of not becoming themselves and becoming themselves most fully. The cold pressure exerted upon things to work themselves out ensures that those things accomplish their own nature – that is the troubling fecundity and obscure goodness of winter. The chill menthol of the air soothes me, freezes out the mind's dirt. Ice and frost and pale light are the elements of alertness, I walk on alert as an antlered deer, tense and yet relaxed in the pull of the winter wood that takes on the current of Latchmore Brook that runs through the wood's centre. Everything flows, shimmers. Let me be not a dam in the flow.

I do not grow tired as I walk for hours following the fascinating rush of Latchmore Brook as it careers out of the wood and into the hollow of the open heath. Poorness and bareness everywhere. Brittle heather and cracked soil budding nothing. Not a sound. Even the lone deer bolting and bouncing off into the land's dream of breath, broad fog and rising mist, is disturbingly quiet.

What richness can I bring, what power? Better to be nothing like the rest, to take part in the pregnancy of spring, and the birth. I let winter rule. I am nothing but my slow breath blending into the ghostly air, a bleak and accepting awareness. A single moment of this becomes my world. Winter yields hardly any life, and yet, when experienced at the level of the soul, it is life itself.

≈

One moonlit white horse clunking along the road beneath the stars. The sound of it, and the sight, goes deep inside me. My whole being echoes the sight and sound, and the silence between each hoof as it falls upon the tarmac then lifts for what seems, in those moments, like eternity. I watch the white horse as it goes into the darkness of the wood that borders the side of the road. The white horse, moonlit, shines out as though the moon shifted into the shape of this horse and took the earth as its abode.

≈

Six roe-deer, perfect and sleek, in cold silks of mist spring up from frosted crowds of bracken. They are so quiet I have to hold my breath to hear them weave themselves back into the morning silks of the heath. One roe tears itself out of the mist, a smooth edged rag of the fabric that held the others intact, and stopped in the middle of the wide heath, upright, alone, and alert. Her alertness and instant wariness at my presence was both alluring and repellent. I was something that she immediately perceived as an outright threat. What was alluring by her behaviour was that she did, in fact, perceive that my presence was confirmed in her sight. Her sight brought me to the moment. For her to bring me into life I must've already been present in some minor, seedling way. Flowering under her gaze, I was a mere seed before her attention. The obscure relation continued until she looked away on her own accord and was left to experience my own coming-to-be before I regressed once again into a lesser but necessary state of being. Where she stood looking askance, the mist left her in a clearing of cold sunlight that touched her tentatively as though the light were enough to break her. But she was strong, and the sunlight flooded upon her and she suddenly fled, darted away across the heath, out of sight but not out of mind.

≈

Second frost of the year, and birdsong echoing through Franchises wood like reverent voices muttering in a church. Fog fainting across the land, laying down in heaps upon the heather. No wind revives the blended bodies of the fog, they stretch their hands across the whole heath, groping in their fainting until they fall and seep into the heather, become ghosts that blind the sun from the earth.

≈

A house of light this morning, the inside brickwork made luminous by the sun pouring in, stirring the dust up in golden clouds that danced in the draft coming in from a crack in the door. I walked slowly from room to room as though through a gallery of light, a living museum of my own, not yet relegated to the dead-end of those morgue-museums in which stale light falls upon somnolent eyes. My shadow rode up the walls, flickered around corners. Facing east, the dining room, bedroom, and kitchen glowed. The house was undergoing the transformations of dawn, the possibilities of another day. The west side of the house remained in shade, as yet untouched by that ancient fire. I wash the dishes and bowls in the light, the golden water pours through my fingers, down my fore-arms, dripping at my elbows.

Stepping outside I put my ear to the wood as though to a shell, hearing one long note of a bird that entwined with the dawn. The light and song echoed through my bones, the song of light was the beat in my heart that the earth made, and the spirit blew the spark into the heart for safekeeping.

≈

One raven croaking southward over the heath that turned from gold to pale grey as the sun was covered with a grey sheet of cloud by afternoon. Three forceful croaks from the raven, then silence. The silence that is the end of his call occupying the land for a while. No wind. The quiet black figure riding over my head. I stand and watch, brought to attention by the raven that doesn't intend to grab my attention but does anyhow. I obey its command of being. Is that all there is to it, just looking? What will hatch forth if I look for so long that my eyes grow dim with fatigue and must rely on the raven's eyes to see? How do you share more deeply in its life and thus move towards a fervent union with things, a union supported by the earth, animated by the Spirit?

≈

Many deer down in Studley Wood beside Latchmore Brook, nosing the hard ground, turning over the crisp leaves with their black noses, their ears flicking and twitching even though there is no sign of a nuisance of flies. One white roe amongst them, cast in a dream of moonlight. I behold him. Do the others behold? He does not seem real amongst their shades of brown. They all pelted off once I began to approach; the white one was the first to go. Save for the white doe, were these the same ones I saw yesterday grazing higher up on the heath? Heaving and striding forward like athletes, they bound across a narrow clearing and resume, far from my human form carved from the vagaries of threat and fear, nudging the ground, nibbling the stubble. Their stillness in the clearing is as exciting as their sprinting across the heath. Their silence, too, is a part of them, and their quiet sounds. How is it that the implacable stare of an animal such as this can be more enticing than a being that blatantly wants you? What is this unrequited fervour that circulates back and forth between myself and the deer? What unwritten law betroths us?

≈

In the entangled woodland of time there are hollows, clearings, as natural as the woodland itself. Continuous with it. One comes across them, steps into them unexpectedly. If I knew how to find them, read the map of the wood, of time, more thoroughly, read between the lines of leaves and branches as it were, then I would be led into more of those clearings, those breathing places of the Spirit, a lit spot of eternity amidst what grows and fades. In one of those clearings, Hope Cottage was built. My roof is a tile-work of clouds, leaves, and stars.

≈

Low-light lit boughs of Studley Wood. Cold, golden air. A treecreeper flurried up an ash trunk, soundlessly merging into ivy. I breathed in fistfuls of dead leaves, again, again, and again. It was as though in that bouquet of last year's autumn leaves I inhaled the sweet and damp aroma of every forest and wood on earth.

≈

The crow was a black fruit in the bare hawthorn as I ran past him in the rain at dusk. Rain blurred my sight. What about his? He looked my way, but very briefly. I looked back and gazed into his darkness. The hawthorn roared in the first powerful gust of evening as though a spirit moved over the land, shaking him off the trees gnarled twigs. For once, I thought, it wasn't I that flushed him from his perch. Or was the gust saving him from my darkness, the human nightfall of names, ego, and control?

≈

Full moon high above the eastern face of the house, the house's face glowing in moonlight, its head amongst the stars. The air as still and as full as the moon, and as quiet. A rising rustle of new leaves in Franchises Wood deepens and strengthens the glowing silence. I stay where I am, two steps out from the back door I leave open to the night. I hear and listen to my breathing become strange and fascinating like the moonlight that flows down my open throat. How far down does it reach? What dark parts are blessed, awoken? It tastes of nothing, and yet something more than anything seen, a colour felt, not merely seen; an emptiness wider than anything

I had supposed. The cold night gets to me, so I take one last look at the night and head on into the house full of an emptiness that embraces and releases every star, brick, eye, and flower into the world. Full moon through the window: my companion of big and glowing stillness.

≈

At times an opaque wind blows between me and the world – an opaque stream of air that is less than air but still of a substance, moving air that is like the blueprint of wind – that maintains an agonising distance between what I have become and what I truly am. In the wind I see a range of earthly things tearing continuously past. They glow with an obedience to the blow in which they are caught and summoned to somewhere holy and beautiful and true. That somewhere, though, is not elsewhere. It is here. The reason why there is a distance between myself and the world through which this wind blows is because I am not here. I am elsewhere. The task, then, is to withdraw from elsewhere, get here, and stay. Then the distance between myself and the world disappears and I, too, take part in the wondrous rush of time as it relaxes into eternity, and the place in which each thing has its own place, a home. I experience this vision because Hope Cottage, not just the building, the garden, the bordering woods, but the sense of belonging upon which Hope Cottage was first of all built, has come to the fore, has risen up through the brickwork and the bare apple-blossom tree. Belonging is of the land itself. This house is built upon a sacred site. An inclusive mystery haunts here.

≈

The wind rattles the letter box, whistles through it into the house, bringing winter indoors. From inside I can tell apart the sound of the wind through the tall twin pair of oaks, and the dense holly. I am not shut out from things in this home. I'm still able to pursue my radical and yet simple aim of becoming more and more a part of things, and in no way, so far, does this dwelling impede upon that.

I think it even encourages and supports it. In this vein a home so easily becomes a kind of monastery or sacred building for practitioners of belonging to be sheltered and protected in their practises of contemplation, practises that range from crushing away dead leaves from the doorstep and sitting in quiet listening to the wisdom of this house and the ground upon which it's built and the starry sky which the roof rises to greet.

≈

Setting sun, circle of yellow, orange, and red flames nestled in the bare oak from where I stood. The oak pursed the sun. Thunder and rain, swipes of lightning across the heath. The sun was the oak's heart, fire and flame in the skeleton, the oak rooted in earth, reaching up to the stars. Incredible. I won't forget today, this evening, how the oak held the sun in its centre and my soul, some deep-seated centre, caught on fire with joy and calm.

≈

First skylark of the year ascending into the first bright warmth of the year. Blue and bright all day. Two buzzards soared over Franchises Wood while I chopped a fallen oak with an axe my father gave to me years ago. It used to be heavy in my hands, now it seems light. Above, the two buzzards mew and wail. I rested the axe down to watch and listen to them fill the sky with their shape and call.

≈

Do we not all need time to relax our grip upon the world in order to sink back into the arms of where we are?

≈

The wind is an invisible fire without light and heat, the mould from which fire is shaped during the elemental boil in the cauldron of earth's first creations. It wildly spreads, engulfing the wide and long heath and the curious night-depth, imageless yet full of traces of the world's first glory, the first wind, billowing over black ponds and around this house in which I sit. I listen as though I were listening to my own pulse, closer to me than my own pulse. Indoor lamps flicker. Things creak like old doors on older hinges, almost breaking. Porous world.

≈

I wandered across the garden this morning to see how the snowdrops were fairing after last night's downpour of wind and rain. They fare well, strong and bright and vivid green stems, very white in the sun and in the shade. They verge on intangibility as I touch them. Snow-flesh, white lamps on green crooks nodding in my breath. I stand amongst them for a while, absorbing their colour and clean delicacy. Lanterns of contemplation. I long to meditate amongst them beneath the moon.

The simple magic of life comes to me when I am most at rest and at ease in the immediate silence of the passing moment, wherein the shadows of snowdrops flicker upon the echoing chamber-walls of the heart.

≈

I will run with the deer after a good night's rest in the arms of Hope Cottage, as they weave and sew themselves in and out, in and out through the sun. Treading heather that springs up the heel as the heel lifts, cantering into dusk, into night and vanishing beyond this human shape that is both blessing and bane.

≈

The oak that arcs above the garden breathes and heaves its body forward from root to sky in the air of the thickening night fog. Animal-like, creature of bark, sap, and root, fed by soil, sunlit rain, the oak lunges out to catch my wonder or provide the perch for a bird. A solitary curlew cries out over the heath, an eerie sound, the wail of a soul longing for home, finding no solace in its echo. Fog clears, stars are the golden fruit budding the branches. Without this one oak, Hope Cottage, this sacred place, would suffer a blow of loss like a thump into where my stomach is most tender. The oak ensures and guards, as does this home, and myself in my truest moments, the inherent sanctity of things. Such things get so easily ripped away by the wrong kind of actions: actions based on a desire to seize, and not the right actions that are based on a desire to let go, to experience things drifting towards themselves, returning home to themselves. Breathe on, then, old oak. I will act and speak how you wish me to, and by doing so I will firmly come home to this place, the place, in fact, I have never left and have always been.

NOTES

EPIGRAPH

1. N. Scott Momaday, quoted in T. C. McLuhan, *The Way of the Earth*, New York: Simon & Schuster, 1994, p. 409.
2. Douglas E. Christie, *The Blue Sapphire of the Mind: Notes for a Contemplative Ecology*, Oxford University Press, 2013, p. 176.

PREFACE

1. Alex Jacobs quoted in T. C. McLuhan, *The Way of the Earth*, New York: Simon & Schuster, 1994, p. 433.
2. Philip Sherrard, 'The Desanctification of Nature,' in *Seeing God Everywhere: Essays on Nature and the Sacred*.ed. Barry McDonald, World Wisdom, 2003, p.109.
3. Max Oelschlaeger, quoted in *The Sacred Earth: Writers on Nature and Spirit*, ed. Jason Gardner, New World Library, 1998, p. 132.

SELF-REALISATION ON THE KUMANO KODO

1. Zen Master Dogen, *Moon in a Dewdrop: Writings of Zen Master Dogen*, ed. Kazuaki Tanahashi, North Point Press, 1985, pg. 216.
2. Lama Anagorika Govinda quoted in Peter Matthiessen, *The Snow Leopard*, Vintage, 1998, p. 20.
3. Lao-tzu, *Tao Te Ching*,ed. Robert Van De Weyer, The Pilgrim Press, 2000, p. 25.

MOUNTAIN THOUGHTS

1. Nan Shepherd, *The Living Mountain*, Canongate Press, 2011, p. 1.

2. John Muir, *Meditations of John Muir: Nature's Temple*, ed. Chris Highland, Wilderness Press, 2001, p. 121.

SURGES
1. Angelos Sikelianos, *Selected Poems*, trans. Philip Sherrard, Princetown University Press, 1979, First American Edition, p. 3.

ECHOING MARSH
1. Theodore Roethke, *The Collected Poems*, Anchor Books, 1975, p. 214.
2. Ted Hughes, *Collected Poems*, ed. Paul Keegan, Faber and Faber, 2005, p. 663.
3. Simone Weil, *Gravity and Grace*, Routledge London and New York, 2007, p. 42.

FORAGINGS
1. Rabindranath Tagore quoted in T. C.McLuhan, *Cathedrals of the Spirit: The Message of Sacred Places* HarperCollins, 1996, p.93
2. Thomas Merton, *When the Trees Say Nothing*, ed. Kathleen Deignan, Sorin Books, 2008, p. 43.

HOPE COTTAGE
1. Novalis, quoted in Douglas E. Christie, *The Blue Sapphire of the Mind: Notes for a Contemplative Ecology*, Oxford University Press, 2013, p. 102.
2. T. S. Eliot, *Four Quartets*, Faber and Faber, 1959, p. 20.

ABOUT THE AUTHOR

WILLIAM HENRY SEARLE, PH.D., born 1987, in Dorset, UK, is a spiritual ecologist whose work draws on the world's diverse spiritual traditions, philosophy, ecology, and personal lived experience in the outdoors to revive the sense of the natural world as inherently wild and sacred. He holds a doctorate in creative writing and environmental philosophy for which he was awarded a three year studentship to study at the Royal Holloway University of London. *Lungs of My Earth* is his first book.

HIRAETH PRESS

❡ Poetry is the language of the earth. This
includes not only poems but the slow flap of
a heron's wings across the sky, the lightning of
its beak hunting in the shallow water; autumn
leaves and the smooth course of water over
stones and gravel. These, as much as poems,
communicate the being and meaning of things.
We strive to produce works of poetry, whether
they are actual poems or nonfiction. We are
passionate about poetry as a means of returning
the human voice to the chorus of the wild.

www.hiraethpress.com

Lightning Source UK Ltd.
Milton Keynes UK
UKOW02f1336070515

251064UK00004B/322/P